Ancient Peoples and Places

ECUADOR

General Editor

DR. GLYN DANIEL

ABOUT THE AUTHOR

*Born in Washington, D.C., Betty J. Meggers studied archaeology and anthro-
pology at the Universities of Pennsylvania and Michigan, and at Columbia University where she took her doctorate.*

*She served as Instructor at the American University, Washington, in 1950–51,
and has since been engaged in research, except for a period from 1959 to 1961, when
she was Executive Secretary of the American Anthropological Association. Since
1954 she has been a Research Associate of the Smithsonian Institution.*

*In collaboration with her archaeologist husband, Clifford Evans, Dr Meggers has
carried out archaeological surveys and excavations in several parts of lowland
South America, including four seasons of fieldwork in Ecuador.*

*She is the author of numerous publications on South American archaeology and
cultural theory, her special interests being cultural ecology and cultural evolution.*

Ancient Peoples and Places

ECUADOR

Betty J. Meggers

76 PHOTOGRAPHS
42 LINE DRAWINGS
5 MAPS
3 TABLES

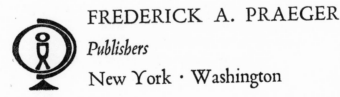

FREDERICK A. PRAEGER

Publishers

New York · Washington

THIS IS VOLUME FORTY-NINE IN THE SERIES
Ancient Peoples and Places
GENERAL EDITOR: DR. GLYN DANIEL

BOOKS THAT MATTER

*Published in the United States of America
in 1966 by Frederick A. Praeger, Inc.,
Publishers, 111, Fourth Avenue,
New York 3, N.Y.*
*Copyright 1966 in London, England,
by Thames and Hudson, Ltd., England
Library of Congress Catalog Card Number: 66-18341
Printed in Great Britain*

CONTENTS

ILLUSTRATIONS

8

9

Preface

As next-door neighbour to Peru, Ecuador has been overshadowed since the Conquest. Tales of wonders and rich booty lured first adventurers and more recently archaeologists to the south, the centre of the greatest empire in aboriginal America. By-passed by the major chroniclers until after the indigenous cultures had fallen into decline, and without a native system of writing, Ecuador depends on archaeology for reconstruction of its prehistory. The record is very incomplete, in part because relatively little work has been done, and in part because of the deleterious effects of the tropical climate.

Although Ecuador provides a wide variety of environments, none is conducive to the preservation of perishable materials. There are no perennial deserts like those in Peru, and dry rock shelters of the kind that have provided evidence of early agriculture in Mexico have not been investigated, if they exist. Only a rare combination of circumstances preserves a piece of wood or cloth, and for an archaeologist to find such an object is an unusual stroke of luck. When one considers that under normal conditions, only metal, stone, pottery, shell and bone will survive, one must also reflect on the small proportion of objects that can be expected to be made from such materials. So what confronts the archaeologist in Ecuador is not the skeleton of an extinct culture, but only a few disarticulated bones.

This situation partly accounts for the fact that most of what is known of Ecuadorian archaeology is the handiwork of two Ecuadorians. The first was Jacinto Jijón y Caamaño, whose investigations were concentrated in the highlands. Working in the early decades of this century, when many modern techniques of excavation and analysis were as yet undeveloped, some of his inferences are subject to revision on the basis of present knowledge. However, these basic data, published in numerous books and articles, remain the principal source of information on the highlands. The second was Emilio Estrada, who began in 1953 to investigate the archaeology of the southern coast. His enthusiasm resulted not only in a prodigious amount of work on his own part, but served as inspiration to others. Most importantly, like Jijón y Caamaño, he recognized the necessity of publication and founded his own monograph series in order to report his results. His unexpected death in 1961 cut short a research programme of remarkable productivity, which in a few short years had caused re-examination of some widely accepted postulates about New World cultural development.

While Ecuadorian archaeology is still too poorly known for a definitive summary to be written, enough data have accumulated to justify stock-taking, both to catch a glimpse of the emerging picture and to identify the principal gaps remaining to be filled. Many of the facts and inferences contained herein derive from unpublished fieldwork conducted in collaboration with Emilio Estrada and Clifford Evans between 1954 and 1961 on the Ecuadorian coast. The attempt to align highland complexes with the coastal period framework has required revision of some of the published sequences and the adoption of period names of broader scope than those in current use. Since facts do not speak for themselves, recourse has been made to modern anthropological theory to give them meaning. The limited compass of this book does not allow detailed presentation of the evidence on which many correlations and inferences are based, with the result that they take on a misleadingly dogmatic tone. It should be remembered that this is only a 'progress report', and that in Ecuador as elsewhere in the world, some of the most significant questions about cultural development are not only as yet unanswered, they are only beginning to be asked.

B.J.M.

Chapter I

Introduction

GEOGRAPHICAL SETTING

Fig. 1

Ecuador fits like a keystone into the arch of the north-ern Andes, between Colombia and Peru. In many cli-matic, topographical and vegetational respects, it is a transition zone. Its coast links Pacific Colombia, the area of highest rain-fall on the continent, with the rainless Peruvian desert, the driest place in South America. Its highland valleys are warmer than those of intermontane Peru but more temperate than those of Colombia. Only over the eastern lowlands does the levelling sameness of the Amazonian forest blend the modern nations of Colombia, Ecuador and Peru into trackless homogeneity.

In a sense, all paths lead to Ecuador, whether they are ocean currents, river drainages or the intermontane valleys of the Andes. Offshore, the north-westward flowing Humboldt Cur-rent meets and mingles with south-eastward flowing currents of warmer water, forming a complicated pattern but with the major impulse tending westward along the equator. Inland to the north, the ramp-like Magdalena and Cauca valleys provide an easy route from the Caribbean coast to the Ecuadorian high-land basins. The upper tributaries of the Marañon and rivers flowing south-west to the Peruvian coast are corridors of access to and from the south. Other large rivers drain from the high-lands toward the vast Amazonian lowlands on the east. All have channelled influences from near and distant places into Ecuador, as well as in the opposite direction, from the time of man's first entry up to the present day.

To characterize Ecuador as transitional implies the existence within its boundaries of strongly contrasting environments. It is, in fact, one of the most heterogeneous zones of the hemisphere, in which almost all combinations of climate and elevation can

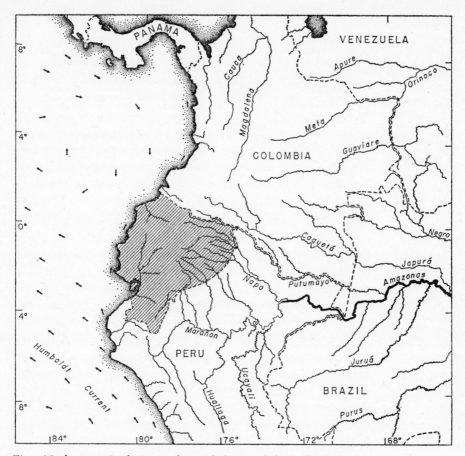

Fig. 1. North-western South America showing the location of Ecuador (hatched area)

be encountered. In general terms, three major segments can be recognized: an eastern and a western lowland separated by the Andean mountain wall. The facts that the Andes are narrower and the coastal plain wider here than elsewhere on the continent, together with an equatorial location, give Ecuador a unique combination of environmental characteristics that certainly contributed as much as its geographical location to the role it has played in New World prehistory.

Fig. 2

17

Of the three major zones, only the Oriente or eastern low/
land is relatively homogeneous in climate, topography and
vegetation. Although the cordillera wall is slightly less precipit/
ous than on the western slope, the numerous rivers that descend
from the intermontane basins cascade through deep and rocky
gorges. At the confluence of the Río Coca with the Río Napo,
the Andes are already out of view and the horizon is the river
bank. Consideration of the infinitesimal gradient that this per/
mits over the remaining 3300 kilometres to the mouth of the
Amazon makes the strength of the current even in the dry sea/
son seem remarkable. Such is the vastness of these rivers that
when water level is lowest steamers can ascend the Napo to the
mouth of the Yasuní and the Putumayo to the foot of the
Andes.

Much of the region today remains trackless forest, the condi/
tions that produce an almost unparalleled diversity in flora
having the opposite effect on settlement by man. The inhibiting
factor is not temperature, which maintains an annual average
between 16 and 24 degrees Centigrade (61 and 75 degrees
Fahrenheit), but the combination of heavy rainfall, low run/off
potential and flatness of the terrain. Between April and Octo/
ber, when the rains are in fullest force, inundation shrinks dry
land to a few scattered islands, making the region less habitable
for game that might contribute to human subsistence. Farming

Plate 8
possibilities are also adversely affected, since exposed soil is
rapidly leached of nutrients. Fish, with almost infinite space in
which to forage, are little tempted by bait and too dispersed to
net profitably.

Although comparable to the Oriente in general elevation, the
coastal lowland contrasts sharply in most other respects. It is the
broadest Pacific coastal plain of South America, expanding
from a width of about 30 kilometres at the Peruvian border to
about 200 kilometres at the Santa Elena Peninsula, and then
tapering down to about 50 kilometres in width at the Colom/

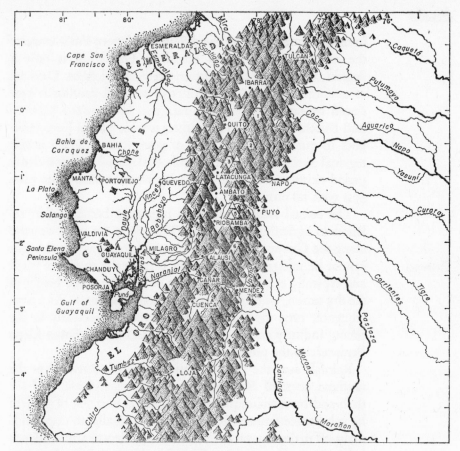

Fig. 2. Some of the principal rivers, towns and other geographical features of Ecuador. Mountains cover areas where the elevation exceeds 1000 metres. Snow-capped peaks are as follows: 1. Cayambé; 2. Antisana; 3. Cotopaxi; 4. Chimborazo; 5. Tungurahua; 6. Sangay

bian border. The basins of the Guayas, Esmeraldas and Santi-ago drainages, less than 200 metres above sea level, form a nearly continuous network of inland waterways.

Plate 1

Except for the Colonche Hills, which rise above 1000 metres, the elevation of the coast is typically less than 500 metres. This, coupled with the equatorial latitude, creates uniformity in temperature such that the difference between the average of the coldest and the hottest month at Guayaquil is only 3 degrees, while the daily variation averages 8 degrees. Days are of uniform length and the principal seasonal contrast is pro/duced by rainfall. Although rain can be expected between mid December and mid May, there is wide annual fluctuation both in quantity and duration of precipitation. There is also regional variation, from the Andean slope where no real dry period exists to the Santa Elena Peninsula, where some years pass with no rain at all.

The coastal rainfall pattern is important because of its re/lation to agricultural potential. The effects are most decisive along the Guayas and southern Manabí coasts, where drought cannot be mitigated by irrigation because the rivers are small and typically contract into a series of puddles at the height of the dry season, when water is most needed for crops. As a con/sequence, even today this area is devoted principally to the fishing industry and to cattle raising, and on the Santa Elena Peninsula to the production of salt.

Rainfall over the Guayas basin and north/eastward to the northern coast of Manabí is ample for agriculture, and the slash/and/burn technique is still employed in much of the area by subsistence farmers. Rising rivers are unable to cope with drain/off in the Guayas basin, which is subject to annual flood/ing in its southern portion. This situation is now exploited by rice farmers, who produce two harvests a year. In pre/Spanish times, however, flooding limited the land usable for crops, since neither manioc nor maize tolerates submerged conditions. At the height of the dry season, when drought parches the land, sloping river banks may have been farmed as they are today along the Río Daule. Pineapples and papayas grow large and delicious, but commercial exploitation has been concentrated on sugar cane, coffee and bananas, all introduced since the Conquest. Guadua bamboo, today widely used for building, either whole as posts or flattened into boards for walls and floors, and balsa wood, whose lightness and durability makes it ideal for raft construction, are coastal forest products. Fibres are provided by wild kapok, cotton and agave.

Along the whole coast, but particularly from Manta south-ward, fishing is the principal focus of life today, providing the main source of income as well as the daily food supply. From Playas, north-west of Posorja on the southern Guayas coast, one-man balsa rafts set forth before dawn to disappear over the horizon, returning hours later with their catch. Near Valdivia, 20 or more men spread large nets and drag them toward shore, surrounding and trapping the fish. White sea bass, sail- and swordfish, róbalo and tuna are among varieties exploited com-mercially. Shell-fish and crabs are gathered on tidal flats and in mangrove swamps.

Plate 58

Terrestrial fauna is less prolific. In spite of modern settlement and competition from cattle, however, deer are still encountered on the Guayas coast. The wilder forested hills of Manabí shelter pumas and a multitude of less formidable species of tropical mammals. Birds are the most abundant form of potentially edible wild-life, ranging from graceful white herons to ducks and doves, the latter in flocks of thousands. Pelicans in single-line formations are a frequent sight offshore, but there is no evi-dence that they were considered more edible in pre-Spanish times than today.

Three islands lie close to the shore. Puná, in the Gulf of Guayaquil, is the largest. Its area of 919 square kilometres falls mainly within the arid zone of the neighbouring coast; like adjacent El Oro, low areas are occupied by mangrove swamp. La Plata, 14 square kilometres in area, lies off the southern Manabí coast. Salango, a little to the south, is smallest and nearest the mainland. All three islands suffer from deficiency in fresh water, reducing their capacity to support permanent settlement.

The transition from lowland to highland is abrupt. Within Ecuador, the Andes constrict to a belt only 70 kilometres wide but averaging 3500 metres in elevation and including 16 permanently snow-clad peaks. There are some 30 volcanoes of the explosive type, which may remain dormant for centuries between bursts of violence. The snow-clad cones of Chimborazo (6310 m.), Cotopaxi (5943 m.), Cayambe (5840 m.), Antisana (5756 m.), Sangay (5323 m.) and Tungurahua (5087 m.) loom skyward with deceptively silent majesty. Their unpredictability is exemplified by Cotopaxi. The first recorded eruption in 1534 was followed by more than 200 years of quiescence. Renewed violence between 1742 and 1768 laid waste to the fertile province of Latacunga. After 109 years of rest, another series of eruptions took place between 1877 and 1880. Cotopaxi has since remained tranquil, but no one can predict how long this state may last.

Fig. 2

The towering height and remote location of most of the volcanoes makes them less a scourge to man than the jarring violence of earthquakes. The Ecuadorian Andes form part of one of the world's great earthquake belts, and tremors of cataclysmic intensity recorded since European settlement form a striking list. Quito has been partially destroyed four times, most recently in 1859 when all the churches lost their towers and many other buildings collapsed. Riobamba was levelled twice, the destruction of 1797 being so complete that it was refounded in a new location. Ibarra, Otavalo, Ambato and Latacunga have all suffered nearly total devastation at least once, the catastrophic 1868 earthquake laying waste to the entire province of Imbabura. In spite of this, there is no evidence that today or in the past this region has been shunned by man. The advantages of fertile soil and temperate climate weigh far more heavily on the scale of survival.

Ten intermontane basins of varying size lie between the eastern and western cordilleras. Their elevation of between 2200 and 2800 metres tempers the equatorial latitude to produce a mean temperature between 13 and 16 degrees Centigrade (55 and 61 degrees Fahrenheit). Although daily variation averages 18 degrees at Quito, the difference between the average temperature of the warmest and coldest month of the year is only 2 degrees Centigrade. There is a drier season between June and September, but seldom is a month completely rainless. Average annual rainfall is between 600 and 900 mm. (28 and 35 inches), sufficient to support natural forests up to about 3400 metres. Above this elevation begin the damp and chilly páramos, high-altitude prairies that occupy the barriers between intermontane basins and coat the mountain slopes up to the snow line. Although potatoes can be grown in sheltered localities, exploitation of the páramo is largely restricted to grazing. Now sheep and cattle replace the llama herds of pre-Spanish time.

The intermontane basins, although varying in fertility, aridity and temperateness of climate, have been characterized as among the most ideal human habitation zones in the world. Maize does well on the valley floors and lower slopes, while potatoes flourish at higher elevations, up to the páramos. The locus of potato domestication is still unknown, but the survival of wild varieties in the Ecuadorian cordilleras places them within the area of possible origin. Other cold-tolerant plants making important contributions to the diet are quinoa (*Chenopodium quinua*), white carrot (*Arracacia esculenta*) and three kinds of tubers: oca (*Oxalis crenata*), melloco (*Ullucus tuberosus*) and mashua (*Tropaeolum tuberosum*). Squash and various kinds of beans are among other indigenous crops. In the warmer climates of the lower valleys, avocados, guavas, chirimoyas, tomatoes and other fruits can be raised. Agave is planted for fibre. Guinea-pigs and llamas were kept in Inca times and probably earlier.

Geographically, Ecuador thus occupies a focal point. Drifting craft from south or north might be cast upon its shore by

Plates 6, 7

ocean currents. The intermontane corridors of Colombia form a ramp to its highland valleys, which are in turn accessible via easy passes to the Peruvian highlands or coast. This Andean route was the one most travelled during the colonial period and corresponds to the course of the Pan American Highway today. The Napo, which funnelled Orellana and subsequent explorers into the Amazonian lowlands, could have served along with other large rivers to channel earlier colonists in the same direction.

The Ecuadorian coast, strategically placed to receive travellers from afar, is also far better endowed to sustain chance arrivals than the perpetually dripping forests of Pacific Colombia or the barren desert of coastal Peru. The exploitation of extreme environments calls for a degree of specialization not demanded on the Ecuadorian coast, which offered something for almost everyone, whether shell-fish gatherer, fisherman, hunter or agriculturalist. The intermontane basins, which serve as a meeting ground between altiplano flora of highland Peru and subtropical vegetation of highland Colombia, may have played a significant role in the domestication and dispersion of certain plants in addition to providing favourable conditions for their later intensive cultivation. The use man has made of such environmental opportunities is the story archaeology has to tell.

CHRONOLOGICAL FRAMEWORK AND TERMINOLOGY

Close collaboration between the few people engaged in archaeological investigations on the Ecuadorian coast over the past decade has permitted adoption of uniform cultural and period terminology. By methods of analysis paralleling those employed by biologists in recognizing species, the attempt has been made to differentiate between local variation in sites representing the same culture and variation that can serve as a basis for

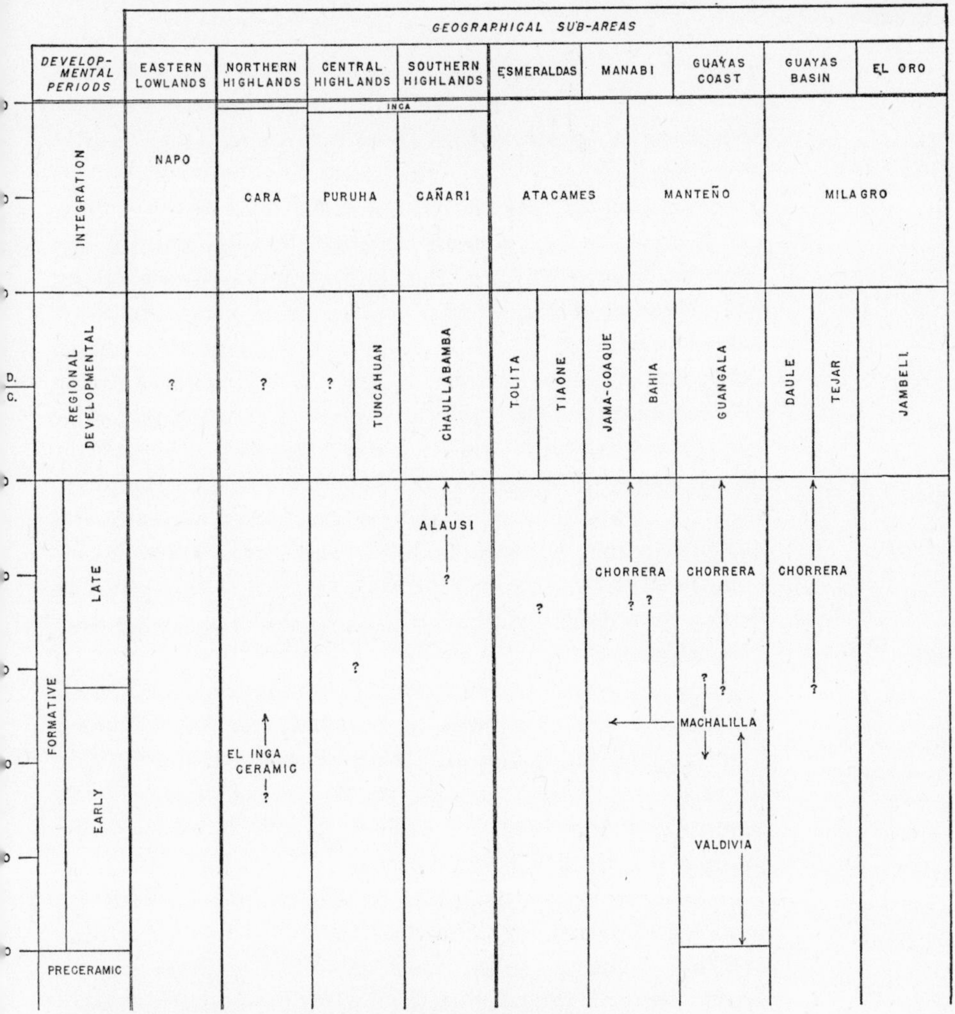

DEVELOPMENTAL PERIODS		EASTERN LOWLANDS	NORTHERN HIGHLANDS	CENTRAL HIGHLANDS	SOUTHERN HIGHLANDS	ESMERALDAS	MANABI	GUAYAS COAST	GUAYAS BASIN	EL ORO
				INCA						
INTEGRATION		NAPO	CARA	PURUHA	CAÑARI	ATACAMES	MANTEÑO		MILAGRO	
REGIONAL DEVELOPMENTAL		?	?	?	TUNCAHUAN / CHAULLABAMBA	TOLITA / TIAONE	JAMA-COAQUE / BAHIA	GUANGALA	DAULE / TEJAR	JAMBELI
FORMATIVE — LATE				?	ALAUSI ?	?	CHORRERA ? ?	CHORRERA ? ?	CHORRERA ?	
FORMATIVE — EARLY			EL INGA CERAMIC ?					MACHALILLA / VALDIVIA		
PRECERAMIC										

Fig. 3. Chronological chart of Ecuadorian archaeological phases

significant geographical and chronological distinctions. Each name on the chronological chart, therefore, embraces a group of sites occupying a particular geographical area during a de-signated period of time. Local differences can be observed

Fig. 3

25

among the members of each group, but these are overshadowed by a core of diagnostic traits that unite the sites of each archaeological phase and set them apart from other similar groupings.

Like biological organisms, cultural phenomena are constantly changing. As a result, considerable alteration through time can be observed in all the cultural phases. When one replaces another as a result of immigration and colonization, the boundary between the earlier phase and its successor is easy to draw; but when the emergence of a new configuration is the culmination of gradual evolution, there is a period of transition through which subdivision is more arbitrary. In such cases there is room for difference of opinion as to where the boundary should be drawn, but disagreements should be founded on the recognition that classification of archaeological remains into cultures or phases is a device for organizing a vast amount of data in an orderly manner as a basis for inferences rather than an end in itself.

Emphasis on similarities rather than differences accounts for the fact that the 5000 years of Ecuadorian prehistory which followed the introduction of pottery-making are encompassed by no more than three periods. The Formative Period sees the introduction of pottery and then of agriculture, and lays the foundation for future development. During the Regional Development Period, interplay between the initial culture and local environments in a context of relative isolation brings into existence numerous well-defined regional complexes. In the final Integration Period, these regional complexes are replaced by larger culture areas suggesting a different kind of sociopoliti-

Fig. 4. Chart of carbon-14 and obsidian dates available for Ecuador. The year 1950 has been used for conversion of elapsed time to calendar dates. Code numbers and letters identify the following laboratories: I, Isotopes Inc.; M, University of Michigan; P, University of Pennsylvania; R, New Zealand; SI, Smithsonian Institution; W, U.S. Geological Survey; Y, Yale University; no letter, Humble Oil Co.

CARBON-14 DATE		PHASE	PERIOD	PHASE	OBSIDIAN DATE
1390 ± 200	(M-736)	Manteño	INTEGRATION	Milagro	AD 460–1480
1190 ± 500	(W-835)				
1181 ± 51	(P-269)	Napo			
1168 ± 53	(P-347)				
1100 ± 105	(1305)	Manteño			
1030 ± 160	(Y-616)	Cañari?			
AD 850 ± 105	(SI-42)	Manteño			
BC 100 ± 120	(M-1315)	Bahía I	REGIONAL DEVELOPMENTAL	Guangala	340 BC–AD 360
160 ± 120	(M-1319)			Daule	640 BC–AD 360
170 ± 120	(M-1316)			Bahía	400 BC–AD 280
200 ± 240	(W-833)			Tejar	540 BC–AD 460
220 ± 200	(M-734)			Jama-Coaque	400 BC–AD 510
250 ± 240	(W-834)				
350 ± 65	(SI-49)				
400 ± 65	(SI-52)				
480 ± 60	(SI-55)				
575 ± 105	(SI-35)	Chorrera-Bahía			
590 ± 125	(SI-43)				
620 ± 440	(Y-617)	Chaullabamba?			
850 ± 115	(1307)	Chorrera	FORMATIVE	Chorrera	1840–540
1370 ± 170	(SI-107)	Machalilla			
1500 ± 50	(SI-69)	Valdivia Period C			
1969 ± 121	(R-1070/1)	El Inga Ceramic			
2020 ± 65	(SI-78)	Valdivia Period C			
2050 ± 190	(I-557)	El Inga Ceramic			
2090 ± 55	(SI-71)	Valdivia Period C			
2100 ± 200	(W-630)				
2150 ± 140	(M-1321)	Valdivia Period B			
2170 ± 65	(SI-82)				
2190 ± 60	(SI-80)				
2220 ± 140	(M-1318)				
2220 ± 65	(SI-85)				
2240 ± 200	(W-632)				
2270 ± 100	(SI-16)				
2280 ± 100	(SI-18)				
2500 ± 90	(SI-22)	Valdivia Period A			
2500 ± 200	(W-631)				
2530 ± 140	(M-1317)				
2580 ± 55	(SI-83)				
2590 ± 150	(SI-84)				
2670 ± 140	(M-1322)				
3200 ± 150	(M-1320)				
5978 ± 132	(R-1070/3)	El Inga Preceramic	PRE-CERAMIC		
7080 ± 144	(R-1070/2)				

cal organization. Although period divisions are shown for convenience as simultaneous throughout Ecuador, it should be kept in mind that just as in Europe different countries passed into the Industrial Revolution at different times, so some Ecua-dorian regions probably forged ahead while others lagged behind.

Throughout this volume, the archaeological cultures are referred to as 'phases', a term employed widely in the New World because of its lack of ethnographic connotations. We do not know whether archaeological phases correspond to tribes or culture areas among living groups, or to some other kind of entity, and the word 'phase' preserves the ambiguity of the archaeological remains in this respect. 'Phase' is preferred to 'complex', because it refers not only to remains of artifacts, but includes whatever can be recognized or deduced in the realms of settlement pattern, sociopolitical organization, religious prac-tices and other aspects of the once living cultural whole. The term 'complex' is reserved for a group of attributes of pottery, stone, metal or other kinds of artifacts associated with an archaeological phase. Where archaeological remains can be identified with known Indians, the phase may be given their name; otherwise a geographical term is usually chosen, often that of a typical site.

ABSOLUTE DATING

Fig. 4

Thirty-six carbon-14 dates are available for coastal Ecuador, four for the highlands and four for the Oriente. Additional evidence of coastal absolute chronology comes from a large number of dates obtained by measurement of the hydration layer on obsidian, a method still in its experimental stage. Where carbon-14 dates exist, however, there is good agreement, so that obsidian dates for phases without carbon-14 dating are probably acceptable approximations of exact age.

CHAPTER II

The Preceramic Period

IT IS NOT YET KNOWN whether the first people who came to Ecuador followed the intermontane basins or moved along the coast, nor how long ago they came. Even the date of the first discovery of America by man is still a matter of specu-lation. Well-made chipped tools occur in sites dated by carbon-14 to about 12,000 years ago in western North America and 8–10,000 years ago in Argentina and southern Brazil, marking the passage of a cultural tradition from north to south, but there is a growing suspicion that these chippers of fine blades did not find the land uninhabited. A leading North American expert, Alex D. Krieger, is inclined to date the first peopling of the New World to 30–40,000 years ago, a time when the Wiscon-sin glaciation was still near its peak in North America. Evidence consists of fragments of cut bone, percussion-chipped stones and remains of hearths from sites in arid parts of the western United States. Traces perhaps reflecting such an early migration, called by Krieger the 'Pre-Projectile Point Stage', have been found in Colombia, Venezuela, Bolivia, Chile, Argentina, Uruguay and southern Brazil in the form of typologically similar large, heavy choppers and scrapers. Like the North American ones, these South American sites occur typically in arid regions, but none have been dated by carbon-14 so that it cannot be demonstrated that they are of comparable age.

Conclusive evidence of the Pre-Projectile Point Stage in Ecuador has not yet been uncovered, but several clues suggest that more investigation may produce it. Fossils of mastodon, horse and other Pleistocene fauna are known to exist on the Santa Elena Peninsula and in the central highlands, indicating that ecological conditions were suitable for the same large game that roamed North American plains, and implying that techniques employed for subsistence in the area from which migrants would have come would not have required drastic modification. Badly eroded shell deposits at the edge of driedup inlets on the southern Guayas coast may be of human origin. Although preliminary testing has not brought to light any worked or unworked stone, bone or other materials attributable to man, a sample of oyster shell gave an age of 26,900 ± 900 years. Assuming a slight time lag for diffusion from North to South America, this falls within Krieger's postulated PreProjectile Point Stage.

Because of its equatorial location, Ecuador was relatively little affected by glaciation during the Pleistocene. Although extensive studies paralleling those in North America and Europe, are yet to be made, it appears that ice did not normally form below 3700 metres. By comparison, the lower limit of permanent snow today averages 4742 metres on the western cordillera and 4564 metres on the eastern cordillera, with individual glaciers extending down to about 4100 metres. Even allowing for local fluctuations to lower elevations, the intermontane valleys would not have been uninhabitable to man. In fact, a colder climate might have favoured extension of the grasslands over areas forested in more recent times, offering a suitable habitat for the large game that was the principal subsistence resource for the PaleoIndians.

The term 'PaleoIndian' was originated to designate a group of stone tool complexes in the United States characterized by wellmade projectile points associated with remains of extinct Pleistocene fauna such as the horse, extinct bison, mastodon and mammoth, and dated by carbon14 to 8–12,000 years ago.

A number of rockshelters and open sites in South America have also produced stone projectile points, but few are in clear association with Pleistocene fauna or have undisputed carbon14 dates. Assignment of approximate ages to finds is further handicapped by the fact that some of the principal point types differ from those in North America. In highland Ecuador, survey by María Angélica Carluci has brought to light a number of localities with obsidian chips and tools, including projectile points, knives, scrapers, and perforators. The majority occur between the Quito region and the Colombian border. Surface samples are not uniform in content, some sites producing only lanceolate or unstemmed points, others both stemmed and unstemmed, and a few predominantly stemmed forms. Since sites with marked differences in relative frequency of stemmed and unstemmed varieties are within a few hundred metres of each other, such differences presumably reflect differences in age.

The only site that has been intensively investigated is El Inga, on the north-east slope of El Llaló, an extinct volcano some 22 kilometres east of Quito. Robert E. Bell, who conducted the excavations, estimates that the site formerly occupied an area of about 228 by 152 metres. The occupation deposit, less than 60 cm. thick, was excavated by artificial levels in the hope of detecting some changes in the kind of relative frequency of artifacts from bottom to top. Some 80,000 objects, the vast majority chips, were catalogued, but no clear-cut trends of changing popularity were detected. Although fossilized bones of various Pleistocene mammals, including mastodon, camel, horse and ground sloth, have been collected in the vicinity, none are clearly associated with the artifacts.

The most common tools are scrapers, the majority irregularly shaped flakes struck from a core and used without reshaping. A few were retouched by percussion or pressure to improve the cutting edge. A small number of more carefully shaped plano-convex scrapers were fashioned from obsidian or basalt. Unifacial or bifacial flakes classified as knives are abundant. Among artifacts less commonly encountered are perforators or gravers, and burin spalls.

Fig. 5c
Fig. 5d
Fig. 5e

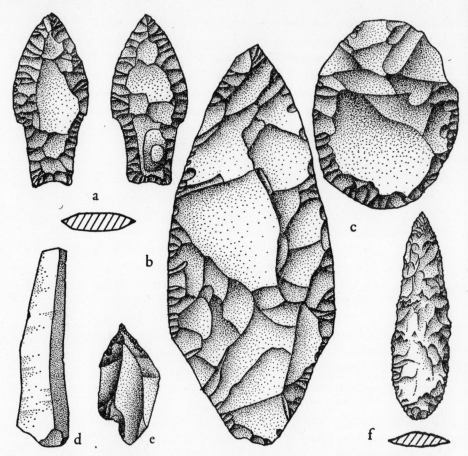

Fig. 5. Stone tools of the Palaeoindian Period in the north Ecuadorian highlands. a. Fell's Cave fish-tail point, El Inga; b. Large ovate point, El Inga; c. Plano-convex scraper, El Inga; d. Flake knife, El Inga; e. Perorator, El Inga; f. El Jobo-like point, Losón

Fig. 5a   Most of the projectile points from El Inga are stemmed. The most distinctive type is referred to by Bell as the Fell's Cave Fish-tail point because of its resemblance to specimens found by Junius Bird at Fell's Cave in southern Patagonia. The Ecuadorian examples differ, however, in having a longitudinal flake removed on one or both surfaces reminiscent of the fluting characteristic of unstemmed North American Clovis points. Another feature shared with Clovis points is smoothing of the basal edges. Some of the ovate points (less common at El Inga than at other highland Ecuadorian sites) resemble examples from El Jobo in western Venezuela, correlated in turn with Santa Isabel Iztapan and Lerma points in Mexico with a carbon-14 date of 9270 ± 500 years.

Fig. 5b, f

If El Inga is correctly identified as an Ecuadorian representative of a southward diffusing Paleo-Indian chipped-point tradition, dates should be slightly more recent than those in North America. In this context, the two earliest carbon-14 dates of 9030 ± 144 and 7928 ± 132 years are close to the expected age.

Although existing information on the Paleo-Indian occupation of the Ecuadorian highlands is neither comprehensive nor detailed, it suggests that the way of life generally resembled that in North America at the end of the Pleistocene. While wandering bands of hunters stalked the horse, sloth and perhaps mastodon on the grassy slopes of the intermontane basins, other small groups of people along the ocean edge must have been foraging for smaller game and shell-fish, and collecting whatever wild plants offered edible parts. This inference is not only justified by evidence that such a way of life existed on the Pacific shore both to the north and to the south, but required to account for an event that occurred around 3000 B C: the introduction of pottery-making to the Ecuadorian coast.

CHAPTER III

The Early Formative Period

FROM THE TIME that pottery-making was introduced until the Spanish Conquest, the record of cultural development in Ecuador is relatively easy to follow. Archaeologists are addicted to potsherds, not because they constitute an outstanding component of the once-living culture, but because they provide unique, extensive and varied evidence from which a multitude of cultural processes and events can be reconstructed. It is fortunate that the most pliable and sensitive category of material culture is also the most abundant and most resistant to the ravages of time.

THE VALDIVIA PHASE

Plate 3

Plate 5

The appearance of pottery is synonymous with the beginning of the Valdivia Phase, named after a fishing village on the northern Guayas coast, where the type site is located. At the time the Valdivia Phase was in existence the salt flats, or salitres, that now occupy broad segments of the coast were filled with shallow water and fringed with mangrove swamp. Sites occupy the borders, easily accessible to the tidal flats and beaches that provided a major part of the food supply. In addition to mollusc, crab and turtle remains, the refuse contains bones from species of fish that do not voluntarily approach the shore, implying that watercraft were used. Fishing equipment included circular hooks cut from pearl oyster shell and notched stone sinkers, perhaps used on nets as they were on the coast of Peru at this time. Deer bones are sufficiently abundant to suggest that hunting was another important activity. The absence of projectile points means that either points were manufactured from a perishable material, or game was snared or trapped.

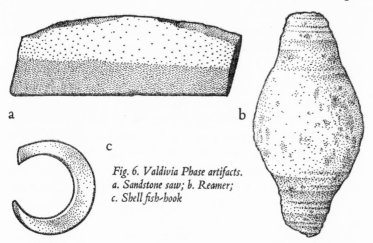

Fig. 6. Valdivia Phase artifacts.
a. Sandstone saw; b. Reamer;
c. Shell fish-hook

Destruction of vegetal remains by the heavy annual rainfall of the Ecuadorian coast makes it impossible to prove that plants were used for food and fibre. However, the fact that coastal Peruvian shell-fish gatherers had been collecting gourds, squash, peppers, lima and jack beans, and had begun to domesticate some if not all of these plants centuries prior to the beginning of the Valdivia Phase makes it a relatively safe guess that similar practices existed among the coastal Ecuadorians. Grinding-stones, useful for crushing seeds, are rare.

The stone, bone and shell artifacts of the Valdivia Phase are with few exceptions manufactured with the minimum effort required to make them functional. Natural stones of suitable size served as hammers. Others were broken to produce an edge that would batter as much as cut. Flakes struck from cobbles were used without further chipping as knives and scrapers. The most standardized objects are sandstone saws with a tapered blade, used for cutting shell, and reamers for boring out the centres of fish-hooks. Tiny blades of chalcedony or opal were used for working bone or antler. Small flakes with graver points may have been employed for decorating bone

Fig. 6a
Fig. 6b

or wood. Among the rarest and best-made stone objects are bowls up to 23 cm. in diameter, pecked from andesite.

In spite of the abundance of deer remains in the refuse at some sites, bone artifacts are rare. Deer antlers with tapered, polished tips may have been used to produce the unusual 'pebble-polished' decoration on the surfaces of some pottery vessels. A few sharpened fish bones could have served as awls. In general, however, both bones and shells appear to have been viewed as garbage rather than as a raw material for the manufacture of tools or ornaments. Of 17,612 shells examined from the Valdivia site, only 23 showed traces of working and the majority of these were fish-hook fragments. A few whole clam shells were perforated for suspension and rectanguloid or tri-anguloid sections were cut from larger shells and made into pendants. Shells were also used as dippers or scoops.

Fig. 6c

The most carefully made artifacts are shell fish-hooks, fash-ioned from disk-shaped blanks of pearl oyster. The outline of the interior edge is almost perfectly circular, while the outer edge is slightly ovoid as a result of increased thickness at the middle of the shank. The tapering point curves toward and nearly meets the bevelled head, which is slightly expanded to prevent the line from slipping off. Valdivia Phase fish-hooks are typically small, ranging between 2·0 and 2·8 cm. in length.

Although preceramic sites with similar kinds of crude stone and shell artifacts have been found on the coasts of Panama, Peru and Chile, all those so far discovered on the Ecuadorian coast also contain competently made and beautifully decorated pottery. Manufacture is by coiling, using sand-tempered paste. Surfaces are even and often polished to a low sheen. Twenty-one per cent of the plain sherds have a glossy red slip. Deco-ration is accomplished by a wide variety of techniques, all of a plastic nature, including incision, excision, appliqué fillet, corrugation, fingernail and fingertip impression, punctation, shell scraping, shell stamping, finger grooving, rocker stamping, drag-and-jab with a multipointed tool, combing, and a fine type of parallel grooving known as 'pebble polishing'. Several techniques are occasionally combined on a single vessel, but variation comes principally from different combinations of sur-face treatment, technique and design motif. Rounded jars with wide mouths and flaring rims, and rounded or angular bowls are typical vessel forms. Bottles do not occur. Except for two kinds of bowls with small tetrapod feet, and occasional jars with well-defined concave bottoms, bases are rounded or slightly flattened. In spite of the high frequency of decorated vessels, there is no evidence that pottery served any but a domestic function.

During the 2000-odd years during which the Valdivia Phase was in existence, a great deal of alteration took place in the ceramic complex. Careful quantitative analysis of strati-graphically excavated samples makes it possible to show that although certain decorative techniques and vessel shapes persist from beginning to end, others have a restricted time span. These *Fig. 7* differences permit the subdivision of the evolutionary con-tinuum into four periods.

The pottery of Period A, 3200–2300 BC, is thick in com-parison to that of later periods, but strong and hard. Both bowls and jars are often red-slipped, but polishing is frequently incomplete on undecorated surfaces. Small tetrapod feet, placed *Plate 9* closely together and truncated by extreme wear, are character-istic of rounded bowls. Bowl rims are unthickened and often undulating or lobed, while jar rims are typically finished by addition of a coil on the exterior, which was finger-pressed at the lower edge to create a scalloped effect. A rare treatment is castellation, in which the rim projects upward or outward at *Plate 10c* four equidistant points. Among decorative techniques, shell stamping is restricted to Period A, while fine-line incision, combing, cutting and bevelling of the rim, finger grooving, *Plate 10k, l, o* fingernail punctation, pseudo-corrugation, and pressing from the interior to raise a row of low bosses on the exterior at the waist are at maximum popularity.

In Period B, which begins about 2300 BC, many of these early forms and techniques survive in declining frequency while others that become popular in Period C make their appearance. Although transitional in nature and of relatively short duration this period is distinguished by maximum popularity of excision, cord impression, multiple drag-and-jab punctation and a bold, somewhat slap-dash variety of incision on an unpolished surface known as Valdivia Incised.

Plate 10a–b,
e–h, k, m, p

By the beginning of Period C, around 2000 BC, the Valdivia Phase ceramic complex has changed markedly from its initial form. With few exceptions, the early decorative techniques have disappeared, and rounded vessels have been replaced by angular-shouldered bowls and cambered-rim jars. Tetrapods are no longer made and concave bottoms are rare. Decoration is principally by nicked rib-and-nubbin appliqué, nicked broad-line incision, rocker stamping, zoned punctation on a red-slipped surface, 'pebble polishing', and texturing of the entire surface with a bunch of twigs or a piece of fluted shell.

Around 1500 BC, when Period D began, the pottery is thinner-walled and less well polished than in earlier periods, and vessels suffer reduction in size. Although pebble polishing and appliqué ribs survive, decoration is typically by incision, including a very broad-grooved form. An unusual kind of finger-pressed appliqué fillet, in which pressure frequently obliterates the fillet at the point of application, becomes popular. Also diagnostic is incision in zones of fine hachure outlined by broader lines.

In addition to containers, pottery was used in the Valdivia Phase for the manufacture of figurines, fragments of which occur in great profusion in the refuse of Periods B and C. Although the earliest examples represent the pinnacle of the

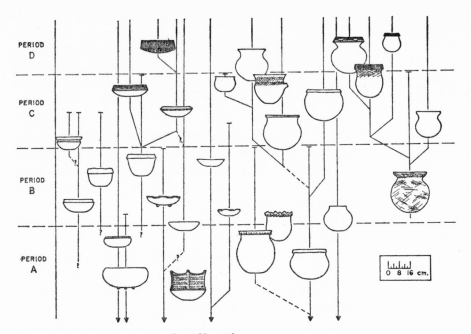

Fig. 7. Vessel shape evolution during the Valdivia Phase

style, suggesting external influence, only tenuous resemblances can be detected to known Formative Period figurines in other parts of the New World, all of which are centuries more recent in date. Workmanship runs the gamut from crude to competent, but the best-made examples are exquisite and elegant in execution. During Period C, evolution follows a trend of decreasing realism, loss of detail and decline in care of workmanship, culminating in the disappearance of the figurine complex in Period D.

The pottery figurines of Period B, designated as the Valdivia type, were modelled by hand on a foundation of two parallel cylinders, joined together through the head and body, then separating to produce the legs. Hair and arms were added by appliqué. On one variety, the arms extend along the sides to

Plate 12

39

join at the front below the rounded breasts. On the other, arms
are reduced to stubs at the shoulder. The back is realistically
contoured, with prominent angular buttocks. In front view,
legs taper toward a blunt end, but in profile a large bulge is
typically present on the back. The body surface is polished
except on the crudest examples, frequently after having been
red-slipped. Significant dimensions are difficult to cite because
of the fragmentary state of most examples. Ten complete torsos
range from 2·0 to 6·3 cm. in length. The smallest head is 1·5 cm.
high, the largest 6·0 cm.

Plate 12

On figurines of the Valdivia type, the hair projects forward
to frame the face. Coiffure is varied and treatment is often
elaborate. The most common hair-style is a long bob, falling
to the shoulders at the front and often to the waist at the back.
The hair surface is decorated with scratch-like incised lines,
sometimes duplicating the natural direction of the hair, sometimes forming geometric patterns or drawn horizontally. A
broad red groove often runs down the centre like a parting, but
occasionally follows an undulating course at variance with this
interpretation. Some heads have normal hair treatment on one
side while the other is 'shaved', red-slipped and polished. Other
coiffures include a braid at the back or at one side, and a large
coil or 'bun' at each side. All of these early pottery figurines are
modelled in the round, with equal attention paid to detail on
the back and on the front.

With the passage of centuries, the figurine style gradually
changed. Bodies became less well finished. Arms were shown
only as shoulder stumps, and ultimately omitted completely.
The face began to project increasingly forwards and the hair
was less carefully detailed. The back was left plain, even on the
head. The hair ceased to be an appliqué addition and was only

Plate 13

suggested by a few incisions, first framing the face (San Pablo
type), later reduced to a band across the top of the head or
eliminated completely (Buena Vista type). Eyes and eyebrows

became longer and more grotesquely curved or slanted, while the mouth disappeared. By the end of Period C, all of the artistry and realism of the earlier examples was lost, and without the complete evolutionary sequence it would be difficult to recognize in these degenerate descendants the original Valdivia type.

Even at the height of their realism, these figurines provide little basis for inference about the appearance of the people who made them. Except for an occasional belt, all are nude. Fine punctation or stippling sometimes covers the pubic area. Rare examples have a patterned red slip suggestive of body painting. Some have bent legs indicating a seated or kneeling position, and a few small zoomorphic objects with flattened tops may be figurine stools. A few are shown holding an infant, but clear indications of pregnancy are extremely rare. More common are twoheaded examples with a common torso. The elaborate coiffures of the earlier type probably reflect similar versatility in hair arrangement among their makers, but the point where realistic representation merges into artistic embellishment is not obvious.

The abundance of figurines implies an important function, presumably of a religious or magical nature. Their interpretation must take account of two important points: (1) the readiness with which even the most carefully made examples appear to have been discarded, which suggests a relatively ephemeral purpose; (2) lack of emphasis on sexuality or pregnancy, although sex is generally female. Both of these characteristics are shared by figurines made by the modern Chocó, Chamí, Emberá and Cuna Indians of northern Colombia. Here, wooden images are used as helpers during curing ceremonies. They serve only once, and when the ceremony for which they were made is concluded, they are thrown away. Being of wood, they soon disappear, leaving nothing for archaeologists of the future to find and speculate about.

Pottery figurines appear only at the beginning of Period B, some 700 years after the inception of the Valdivia Phase. Figurines of Period A are entirely different in style and made of stone. The simplest type, which can be recognized as a figurine only because it forms the beginning of an evolutionary sequence of gradually increasing complexity, is a thin, elongated slab of shale, fine-grained sandstone or mudstone. Some slabs, whose natural form was too wide or asymmetrical, were squared off to produce a rectanguloid outline. Length of this type is between 3·8 and 8·5 cm.

Fig. 8a

Fig. 8b

The first indication of anthropomorphic significance takes the form of an incision or notch at one end, representing legs. A figurine identification is obvious when the upper part of such notched stones bears incision crudely depicting a face and arms. The final form is a stubby and thickened version of the original slab with one surface beautifully incised in short straight lines delineating eyes, nose and mouth.

Fig. 8c, d

Fig. 8e

Fig. 8f

Several sites of Period C have yielded burials. The poor condition of the remains makes posture difficult to discern, but most skeletons lie on their right side with legs tightly flexed and arms extended along the hips. It is probable that the body was wrapped for burial in a mat or cloth, as was the practice on the contemporary Peruvian coast. Tools and ornaments were seldom placed in the grave, but a polished stone axe, a shell scoop or a pottery vessel sometimes occurs. Infants were buried in jars.

TRANSPACIFIC CONTACT AND THE ORIGIN OF
THE VALDIVIA PHASE

The abrupt appearance of pottery on the coast of Ecuador around 3200 BC is an event of more than local significance. Archaeologists have long speculated on the time and place of origin of pottery-making in the New World, modifying hypotheses as fieldwork turns up ever older ceramic complexes in

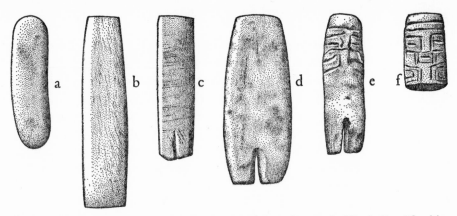

Fig. 8. Stone figurines characteristic of Valdivia Phase Period A. a. Flat natural pebble; b. Shaped flat slab; c. Shaped slab with groove separating legs; d. Thicker slab with legs completely separated; e. Crude face incised at upper end; f. Carefully incised anthropomorphic features covering the front

previously unexplored regions. Contrary to expectation, the earlier the pottery, the better it is made and the less it appears to resemble experimental beginnings of a complicated technology. Valdivia Phase pottery, with an initial carbon-14 date of 5150 ± 150 years (c. 3200 BC), is not only the earliest yet reported in the hemisphere, but the most varied in vessel form and decorative technique of known Early Formative complexes. As such, it can only be interpreted as the result of introduction of a well-developed ceramic tradition from elsewhere. Since both its relatively great antiquity and its unique characteristics appeared to rule out derivation from a New World prototype, the Ecuadorian archaeologist Emilio Estrada looked farther away for similarities. He found many in the Early and Middle Jōmon pottery of central and western Japan. Indeed, when allowance is made for variations that would result from use of different clays and for modifications during learning by people previously unacquainted with the craft, Valdivia pottery is remarkably similar to that of the same age from Kyushu, at the opposite edge of the Pacific. Only one explanation suits all the facts: an accidental transpacific voyage some 5000 years ago from western Japan to the Ecuadorian coast.

Three shell-midden sites on the Japanese island of Kyushu have pottery showing almost all the features present at the beginning of the Valdivia Phase. Two, Sobata and Ataka, are located along the southern margin of the Kumamoto Valley, where the shoreline appears once to have been. The third, Izumi, is in a similar environmental setting on south-western Kyushu. Numerous other Jōmon period sites on the island attest to its long occupation by pottery-making people, whose way of life was otherwise probably very much like that of the fishermen and food gatherers on the Pacific shores of the New World.

Pottery from Sobata, Ataka and Izumi is astonishingly similar to that of early Valdivia. Incised designs on polished or unpolished surfaces present the same combinations of concentric rectangles, zones of parallel lines, and incision alternating with punctation, executed with a tool that duplicates the broad, square-ended grooves typical of Valdivia Broad-line Incised. Early Valdivia Excised designs feature the same crudely gouged-out 'hour-glass' or 'dog-bone' elements seen on Jōmon excised vessels. Bands of fine parallel striations drawn by dragging a piece of fluted shell across the wet vessel surface are characteristic of both, as are more unusual bands or over-all treatment produced by application of the same tool in a drag-and-jab technique. Broader rounded grooves made with the finger are duplicated, as are fingertip punctations, particularly as rim ornamentation. Some of the techniques, especially combing and drag-and-jab punctation, are used for more elaborate, over-all patterns on Kyushu Jōmon vessels than on Valdivia ones, a situation in keeping with a hypothesis of simplification during transpacific transplantation. Other differences can also be fitted into a picture of Jōmon ancestry, among them the incised decoration of Kyushu pottery, in which tech-

Plate 11

Plate 10

niques and motifs of two early Valdivia Phase types, Valdivia Incised and Valdivia Broad-line Incised, are intermingled. The Kyushu incised pottery is, in other words, a generalized ancestor from which the two Valdivia types might easily have differentiated.

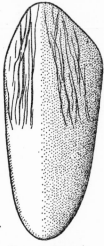

Since stone figurines are present from the beginning of the Valdivia Phase, and since similar objects have not been re-ported from preceramic shell-fish gatherers on other parts of the Pacific coast of America, the possibility exists that this cultural element and whatever practices it reflects were introduced along with pottery-making from western Japan. So far, only a rock-shelter excavated by Teruya Esaka on north-western Shikoku Island has produced anything remotely comparable. At this site, tentatively identified as pre-Jōmon in date, a number of thin, flat pebbles with naturally ovoid to teardrop form have been found, which have faint scratches on one face. Only the general conception is similar to early Valdivia Phase stone figurines; details of execution are different. However, since the unincised Valdivia Phase examples were recognized as figur-ines only after the more elaborate ones were found, it may be that similar unworked pebbles in Jōmon shell middens have escaped attention.

Fig. 9. Natural pebble with scrat-ches on one half suggesting long hair excavated by T. Esaka in a pre-Jōmon site on the Japanese Island of Shikoku

In offering an hypothesis for the introduction of a cultural trait or complex from another area, is it necessary to establish not only that the essential elements exist in the proposed area of origin, but also that they are of equal or greater antiquity there. In this case, carbon-14 dates indicate that Jōmon shell-fish gatherers were making pottery for some 4000 years prior to its appearance on the Ecuadorian coast. During these millennia, vessel shapes and decorative techniques underwent a great deal of alteration. By around 5000 years ago, nearly all of the initial Valdivia ceramic features were present in pottery being made on Kyushu, and many were widely distributed on the other Japanese islands. In fact, the carbon-14 age for one site of this period on Honshu is 5102 ± 400 years, remarkably close to the earliest Valdivia Phase determination of 5150 ± 150 years.

The Jōmon people were probably equally at home on the water and on land, since much of their time must have been spent fishing. Like many present-day fishermen in the Pacific region, they must have been accustomed to exposure to sun and rain, and have known the tricks of satisfying hunger and thirst at sea. Historic records of accidental drifts lasting not only days or weeks but months are so numerous as to suggest that this was by no means an uncommon event in the more distant past.

Added to cultural and psychological factors favourable to the hypothesis of transpacific contact at this early date is the pattern of winds, storms and ocean currents. The currents off the Kyushu coast are among the strongest in the Pacific Ocean, running from 24 to 32 miles per day toward the north-east. In bad weather, typhoons gather their force off the Philippines and sweep past the Japanese islands in a path that frequently coincides with that of the currents. As they peter out, prevailing winds and gales continue in a similar direction, as do currents of lesser velocity. On the usual flattened map, their path looks like a large detour, passing north of the Hawaiian Islands and then curving southward along the American coast. On a globe, however, it is evident that this is the Great Circle route, in actuality the shortest distance between Kyushu and Ecuador, some 8200 nautical miles.

There is no way of knowing how many survivors remained when the Jōmon canoe came to rest on the broad sandy beach of the Guayas coast, and little to suggest their appearance. It is possible, however, that they were more similar physically to the native Ecuadorians than to modern Japanese, whose ancestors immigrated from the Asiatic mainland in more recent times. In any case, these and other individuals cast from time to time upon the shores of the New World are unlikely to have left a detectable imprint on the physical type of the New World population.

What the Jōmon newcomers did contribute was new cultural elements. Of these, pottery is the most obvious because it forms so large a part of the archaeological record. Innovations may also have been made in aspects of the culture that do not sur, vive, for example in mythology, social customs, or arts and crafts employing perishable materials like wood or fibre. Be, cause in both Japan and Ecuador the climate destroys all but the most durable objects, and because these events took place so long before the beginning of written records, imagination can offer many suggestions that reason must reject as not subject to scientific verification.

THE MACHALILLA PHASE

According to available carbon-14 dates, the Valdivia Phase lasted some 2000 years. While the pottery and figurines changed greatly during this time, most utensils of stone, bone and shell remained essentially the same, a reflection of the functional nature of their form and an indication that activities directed toward satisfaction of the needs of daily life persisted largely unchanged.

About the beginning of Valdivia Period C, small amounts of pottery representing a completely different ceramic tradition make their appearance in Valdivia Phase sites. This pottery belongs to the Machalilla Phase, so named after the site on the southern Manabí coast where it was discovered. Machalilla Phase sites occur not only at the edge of former inlets, but also on high cliffs along the present shore. The area of distribution extends farther north than that of the Valdivia Phase, into southern Manabí Province, and the earliest known sites of the Phase are in this northern portion.

As in the Valdivia Phase, the major focus of subsistence was the resources of the sea. Machalilla Phase fishermen used sand,

Fig. 10

stone saws and reamers to fashion their shell hooks, as did the Valdivians, but most of the hooks are much larger. Diameters between 5·0 by 6·5 cm. and 3·5 by 4·0 cm. for the ovoid exterior edge are typical. The shape is generally similar to the Valdivia one, but the zone of greatest width is near the point rather than at the back, and continues to taper off toward the upper end. Ornaments not yet identified for the Valdivia Phase are a narrow bracelet of shell and a carnivore tooth pendant. Cutting implements include the same rudimentarily shaped blades, scrapers, gravers, choppers and hammer-stones used in the Valdivia Phase with one addition: a large, loaf-shaped grinding stone.

Fig. 11

Machalilla Phase pottery differs both in vessel shape and decoration from that of the Valdivia Phase. Among important new forms are bottles with either cylindrical or stirrup spouts. Both bowls and jars typically have an angular shoulder and a rounded or slightly flattened base. Jars usually have narrow mouths and everted rims, and sherd disks may have served as stoppers. In decoration, Machalilla Phase pottery is the earliest in Ecuador to make use of painting. Fine or broad parallel red bands are most common, with the paint so thick that it often

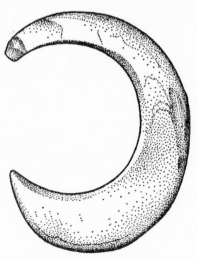

Fig. 10. Shell fish-hook of the Machalilla Phase

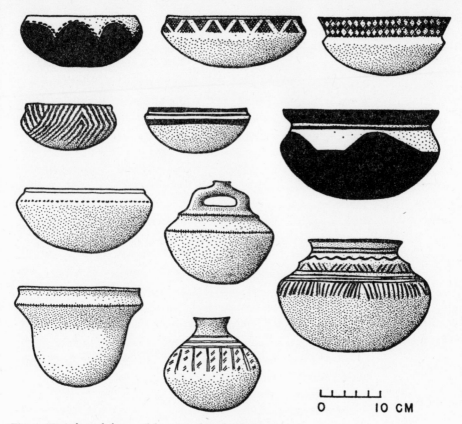

O   10 CM

Fig. 11. Typical vessel shapes and decoration of Machalilla Phase pottery

leaves an easily-felt ridge. Polishing subsequent to painting caused streaking of the edges of the lines. Occasionally, red-painted designs incorporate unpolished zones filled with or bounded by incision or punctation.

Incision, characteristic in the latter part of the Machalilla Phase, is best represented by Ayangue Incised vessels with remarkably thin walls, well-polished surfaces and rectilinear decoration drawn with a pointed tool when the surface was very dry. Motifs include triangles or diamonds filled with parallel hachure, groups of four to six parallel lines slanting in alternating directions, and cross-hatch filling a broad or narrow band above the shoulder. Another common kind of ornament is embellishment of the angular bowl or jar shoulders with a row of nicks, gashes or small bumps. About 20 per cent of sherds are decorated, but as with the Valdivia Phase there is no evidence that these vessels had any but a domestic function.

Fig. 12

In contrast to the Valdivia Phase situation, figurines are very rare. The few fragments that have been found are crudely modelled, with 'coffee-bean' eyes, a prominent ridge-like nose and no mouth or hair. A row of perforations at each side of the head is characteristic. Arms are short projections that break off easily. A few examples have red-banded decoration, but the surface is typically poorly smoothed and undecorated. The rarity of figurines suggests that they may have had a different meaning from those of the Valdivia Phase.

A few burials encountered in excavations of habitation sites indicate that interment in the village probably beneath the house floor was one method of disposal of the dead. Legs were tightly flexed and no non-perishable grave goods occur. In spite of their fragmentary condition, the skeletal remains are of extreme interest because the skulls exhibit marked artificial de-formation, in which the back of the skull is flattened giving the head a trianguloid outline when seen from above.

Like the Valdivia Phase, the Machalilla Phase appears on the central Ecuadorian coast in fully developed form suggesting introduction from elsewhere. Unfortunately, no similar pottery has been found that is old enough to be its source. All known occurrences of the diagnostic traits in the Andean Area are more recent, and can be traced to Machalilla Phase influence. Many elements of vessel shape and decoration are closely dup-licated in Mexico and Central America, but the complexes in which they occur are either undated or assigned to a more recent period, between about 500 and 200 BC. The relatively

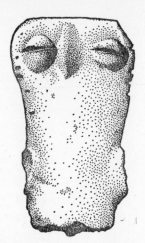

Fig. 12. Fragmentary Machalilla Phase pottery figurine

widespread occurrence of Machalilla Phase traits in Meso⁄america, however, suggests a northern derivation, a speculation that only further fieldwork along the Pacific coast of Mexico and Central America can confirm or deny.

CULTURAL DEVELOPMENT ON THE COAST
DURING THE EARLY FORMATIVE PERIOD

Between 3200 and 1500 BC sedentary life on the Ecuadorian coast appears to have been restricted to the margin of the sea, which provided a reliable localized food supply that could not be equalled inland until after the development of agriculture. On the coast of Peru at this time, the first steps toward plant domestication had been taken. Beans and squash were raised for food, while bottle gourds and cotton were grown to provide raw materials for containers, floats, nets, lines and other kinds of manufactured goods. In all probability the coastal Ecuador⁄ians did the same. Like more recent incipient agriculturists they probably made seasonal or periodic visits to inland regions to collect fruits and other wild plant foods. Men probably spent a good part of their time hunting and fishing, while women and children searched the tidal flats and mangrove roots for molluscs and crabs.

Few clues exist as to the appearance of the village. Fragments of clay with stick impressions suggest that wattle-and-daub huts provided shelter from annual rains. The dead were buried beneath the house floor, probably wrapped in a mat. Few possessions accompanied them to the after-world, perhaps an indication that these people did not view it in a materialistic way.

Kinship ties and reciprocal obligations probably regulated social relations between members of the community. This system, universal among primitive peoples, ensures that no one starves as long as any hunter is successful, that orphaned children will be cared for, and that assistance will be forth-coming whenever an additional pair of hands is needed. The oldest able-bodied man may have been the nominal leader, but his advice would be followed because of his wider experi-ence rather than because he exercised real authority. He may also have been a curer. If the small figurines were used in curing ceremonies, their abundance implies that the Valdivians often needed treatment.

Tools and utensils of shell, stone and bone were shaped only enough to make them functional. More attention was given to the appearance of pottery, a large proportion of which was decorated by a variety of techniques. Both jars and bowls were relatively small, with mouth diameters usually between 18 and 24 cm. suggesting that large quantities of food or drink were not prepared or stored. In addition to what has survived, the people of the Valdivia and Machalilla Phases must have made and used numerous perishable objects, such as baskets, mats, nets, cordage, bags and wooden utensils. When it is remembered that some 60 per cent of the archaeological remains from pre-ceramic sites on coastal Peru are of a perishable nature, the incompleteness of the evidence forming a basis for recon-struction of Early Formative life on the Ecuadorian coast can be readily appreciated.

EARLY FORMATIVE HIGHLAND COMPLEXES

Except for a few sites in Peru, the Early Formative Period is almost unknown throughout the Andean highlands. In Ecuador, carbon-14 dates of the necessary antiquity have been obtained from the upper levels of El Inga in association with badly eroded and predominantly undecorated pottery with generalized Formative characteristics. Only one fragment has a well-preserved surface, which was red-slipped after incision by a broad-ended tool. Although slight, this evidence fits into a picture reconstructed on the basis of more extensive information available to the north and south.

At Kotosh, near Huánuco in the central Peruvian highlands, University of Tokyo archaeologists have recognized five cultural periods. The first pottery, dated to around 1800 BC, is characterized by vessel shapes and decoration present 500 to 1000 years earlier on the northern coast of Colombia. If this tradition moved southward through the intermontane valleys and basins, El Inga would have been along the hypothetical route. The dates from the pottery levels are about 2000 BC, older than the first pottery at Kotosh but more recent than that on the Colombian coast.

If pottery-making diffused southward through the Andean highlands, reaching central Peru by the beginning of the second millennium BC, this is an important fact. However, it implies another fact of even greater importance: the replacement of wild food exploitation by agriculture. Pottery is too fragile and unwieldy to be adopted by people almost constantly on the move, and its appearance generally indicates the abandonment of a wandering existence for a more sedentary way of life.

This sequence of events has been clearly demonstrated in the Mexican highlands by R. S. MacNeish and his co-workers, who have traced the steps from plant collection to plant cultivation in the Tehuacán valley. Almost nothing is yet known about the origin of the principal South American staples, and the poor correlation between hypotheses of botanists and anthropologists and what is now known of the true history of maize domestication suggests that little confidence can be placed on theories relating to the place of origin of potato and manioc cultivation. Plant domestication begins so early in Mesoamerica that the idea could have spread from there to the Andes, where it might have stimulated experimentation with local plants already being exploited in their wild state. The potato, which still grows wild in out-of-the-way spots in the Ecuadorian highlands, is the temperate counterpart of manioc, the staff of life of lowland tropical forest villagers. Whether their histories of domestication are linked or independent is a problem for future archaeologists to solve.

Although archaeological details are few, it seems reasonably safe to assign independent histories to the origin of plant domestication in the Ecuadorian highlands and coast on climatic grounds alone, since plants well adapted to one region do not ordinarily thrive in the other. The almost complete contrast between the products of highland and coastal agriculture in modern Ecuador is a continuing reflection of this environmental dichotomy.

CHAPTER IV

The Late Formative Period

THE TIME WHEN THE mangrove swamps of the Guayas coast began to be replaced by salitres is not firmly estab/ lished, but changes in the distribution of Valdivia Phase sites suggest that the process had reached an advanced stage by around 1500 BC. About this time an event occurred that significantly altered the course of Ecuadorian prehistory and laid the foundation for subsequent cultural development: the introduction of maize cultivation to the Ecuadorian coast.

Although actual maize has not been found, circumstantial evidence of its presence is strong. Maize cultivation is ancient in Mesoamerica, and known to have been practised there by coastal groups whose pottery includes elements making their appearance in Ecuador at this time and signalling the beginning of the Chorrera Phase. Maize becomes a staple in coastal Peru with the introduction of Chavín pottery, which resembles that of the Chorrera Phase and is slightly more recent. Also sug/ gestive is the fact that Chorrera Phase sites are not restricted to the shore, as are those of the Valdivia and Machalilla Phases, but occupy the banks of the Babahoyo and Daule rivers and other interior locations suitable for farming. Potatoes and quinoa, possibly domesticated prior to this time in the highlands, do not grow on the coast. The principal lowland staples are manioc and maize, and maize is the plant associated in Meso/ america with the cultural innovations marking the inception of the Chorrera Phase.

THE CHORRERA PHASE

The majority of known Chorrera Phase sites are either on the
Guayas coast from the Santa Elena Peninsula northward to the   *Fig. 13*
Palmar region, or along the banks of the Daule and Babahoyo   Plate 14

rivers, the principal tributaries of the Guayas. Existing evidence suggests that sites in these two regions are of equivalent age, implying a rapid spread away from the coast where aridity is a handicap to farming toward the more favoured Guayas basin. Although refuse deposits near the shore include marine shell indicating that seafood was not neglected, and the interior rivers were undoubtedly fished, shell fish-hooks and tools for their manufacture are absent. This, as much as the change in settlement pattern, implies a significant alteration in the focus of subsistence.

Small obsidian blades and flakes abound in Chorrera Phase refuse, another sharp contrast with the Early Formative situa-tion. Although obsidian was the preferred material for stone implements in the highlands during preceramic times, it was not employed by people of the Valdivia and Machalilla Phases. Since both the material and the technique of chipping have deep roots in Mesoamerica, their appearance constitutes addi-tional evidence of Mesoamerican contact. As often happened, the Ecuadorians outstripped their teachers, and many of the thin obsidian blades are straight, sharp-edged and as transparent as window glass.

Chorrera Phase pottery varies more widely in wall thickness and surface finish than that of the preceding period, and de-corated vessels constitute a smaller proportion of the total pro-duction. The best-made pottery is remarkably thin-walled, with polished surfaces sometimes approaching mirror sheen. Colour on a single vessel often ranges from buff through red-dish brown to black, reflecting poorly controlled ventilation during firing. Execution is otherwise technically competent, so that although wall thickness is often 3 to 4 mm., sherds do not break easily, and breaks do not occur along coil junctions. Red slip was sometimes applied before polishing, with a result that is difficult to distinguish from red surfaces produced by oxi-dized firing. Well executed polishing occurs on some 56 per

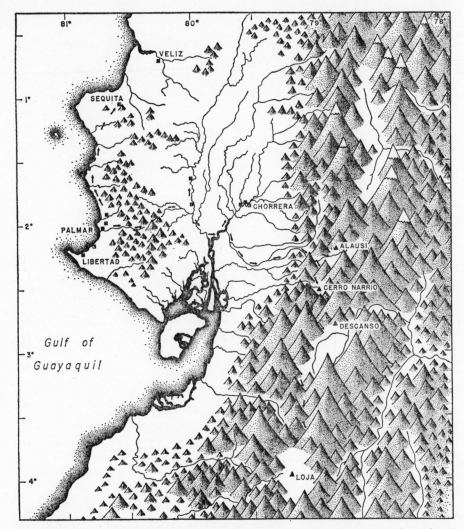

Fig. 13. South-western part of Ecuador showing the location of Chorrera Phase sites on the coast (squares) and of specimens from the southern highlands (triangles) identified with the Alausí Phase

cent of the sherds, while another 25 per cent are incompletely polished leaving horizontal, sometimes widely separated glossy lines.

Decorative techniques reaching maximum popularity at this time are iridescent painting, zoned red painting, burnished lines and polished red rim. Rare but diagnostic are rocker stamping, red and black zones defined by incision, and finely traced incision on highly polished surfaces. Punctation, appliqué rib, and incision on unpolished surfaces also occur.

Plate 15

The most noteworthy element of this complex is iridescent painting. Although still undergoing analysis, the effect is believed to have been produced by application of a thin film of fine-grained clay to the polished surface before firing. All designs are composed of bands of finger width, circles and ovals, suggesting application with the finger. Rarely, iridescent bands are delimited by fine incised lines. This decoration generally occurs on the interior of flaring bowls with rounded or annular bases and level or undulating rims. An incised line often borders the rim interior.

Rocker stamping is always produced with a straight-edged tool, never dentate as is common in other Formative complexes in the New World, and not zoned by incision. Strokes tend to be long and the effect as well as the technique is so different from the characteristic Valdivia variety as to suggest a separate origin. Chorrera Phase examples are exceedingly rare, and application is confined to a single horizontal band on the upper vessel exterior, on an unpolished surface.

Except for iridescent painting, the most striking innovations are in vessel shape rather than decoration. The closed, angular bowls of the Machalilla Phase are replaced by open forms with out-flaring walls and low annular bases 16–20 cm. in diameter. A decorative step or ridge often breaks the evenness of the interior surface where the rim blends into the body wall. A new bottle form appears, with an off-centre cylindrical or tapering spout connected to a bridge handle rising from the base of the spout and terminating in a whistle. Whereas Machalilla Phase spouts have slightly out-turned rims, those of the Chorrera

Fig. 14

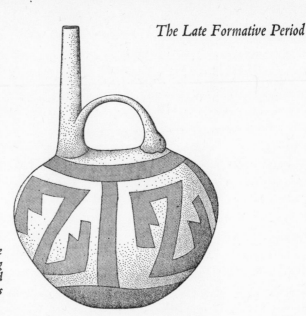

Fig. 14. Chorrera Phase bottle with tapering spout and connecting handle ending in a whistle. Zoned iridescent painting (hachure) covers the highly polished body surface

Phase are either unmodified or have a ring-like thickening. Zoomorphic and asymmetrical forms occur but globular bodies are most common.

A number of beautifully modelled figurine heads of the type called Mate by Estrada have been attributed by him to the Chorrera Phase. Although this association has not been veri-fied stratigraphically, it is supported by a zoomorphic jar on which Chorrera Phase spout-and-handle form and zoned-incised decoration are combined with a head resembling the Mate type. The figurines are hand-made. Smaller examples are of solid construction, with even but unpolished surfaces and a smooth beret-like head-dress. Hollow heads are larger and often sculptured with great artistry. Facial features are similar to those of solid heads, but more symmetrical. The head-dress is more elaborate, with an out-curved border and asymmetrical orna-mentation by incision or excised and polished zones.

A unique artifact diagnostic of the Chorrera Phase is a tubu-lar or 'napkin-ring' ear spool made of fine-textured, highly

Plate 16

Plate 18

Fig. 15a, b

Fig. 15c

Fig. 16

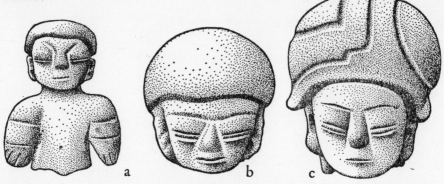

Fig. 15. Mate type figurines possibly associated with the late Chorrera Phase. a. Small solid variety showing body form; b. Larger solid head; c. More carefully sculptured hollow head

polished pottery. The sides are very thin and slightly flaring so that the diameter is 4–5 mm. greater at one end than at the other. The diameter of the larger end ranges from 2·7 to 4·8 cm.; the length is 1·4 to 2·7 cm.

Little is known of the sociopolitical and religious aspects of the Chorrera Phase. The rarity and exquisite workmanship of

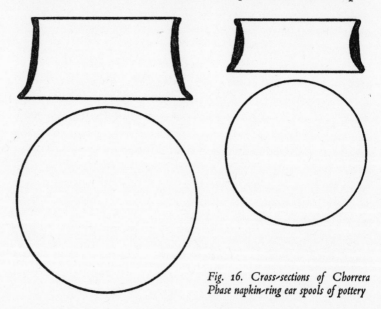

Fig. 16. Cross-sections of Chorrera Phase napkin-ring ear spools of pottery

the napkin-ring ear spools suggests that they may have bene worn only by individuals of high rank. The scarcity of highly polished, thin-walled jars also indicates limited use, perhaps by chiefs, religious leaders or both. Although such evidence of status differentiation is slight and indirect, it is so abundant in the subsequent Regional Developmental Period as to imply that during the Chorrera Phase the initial steps must have been taking place.

MESOAMERICAN CONTACT AND THE ORIGIN OF THE CHORRERA PHASE

A clue to the origin of the Chorrera Phase is provided by the inclusion of several characteristic Machalilla Phase pottery types in the ceramic complex. Most common is Ayangue Incised, done on a polished surface after it was dried hard, so that the incising tool left a slightly ragged-edged line. Other Machalilla Phase techniques are red banding, double-line incision and embellishment of the shoulder with a row of gashes. Bottles and angular-shouldered (carinated) bowls also have Machalilla Phase prototypes.

Fig. 17

When Machalilla Phase survivals are eliminated, several new ceramic traits and two new kinds of artifacts remain to be accounted for. The artifacts consist of obsidian flakes and chips and 'napkin-ring' ear spools. The striking resemblance between the latter and napkin-ring ear spools of Mesoamerica called attention to the possibility of Mesoamerican contact, but its demonstration came only after the discovery by Michael D. Coe of the Ocós Phase, an archaeological culture of approximately equivalent age on the Guatemalan coast.

Most of the Chorrera Phase traits that cannot be explained as Machalilla Phase survivals are present in the Ocós Phase. The principal exceptions, annular bases and napkin-ring ear spools, occur elsewhere in Mesoamerica, and their absence from

Fig. 17

La Victoria, the type site of the Ocós Phase, serves mainly to suggest that the source of influence was a different site. The most outstanding contrast between the pottery of the Ocós and Chorrera Phases lies in the greater delicacy of the latter, Ocós pottery being typically thick and heavy. This difference is traceable to the Chorrera Phase heritage from the Machalilla Phase, the pottery of which is notable for thinness of vessel walls and frequency of polished surfaces.

Fig. 1

The evidence used to postulate Mesoamerican influence is much like that used to reconstruct the transpacific origin of the Valdivia Phase. The same coastal currents that brought the Jōmon canoe to the coast of Ecuador brought the Mesoamericans to nearly the same place. The immigrants must have encountered both Valdivia and Machalilla Phase villagers; why they joined forces only with the latter is a puzzle that may never be solved. Whatever the reason, the Valdivia Phase became extinct, and subsequent Ecuadorian cultures show no traces of its influence.

THE LATE FORMATIVE IN THE HIGHLANDS

An attempt to trace the diffusion of the Chorrera Phase into the highlands runs into difficulties because most archaeological investigation in pottery-producing sites took place prior to the recognition of a Formative Period in the Andean Area. However, several collections of potsherds described by Collier and Murra from the southern highlands incorporate a number of Machalilla and Chorrera Phase elements. A collection from the Alausí basin in southern Chimborazo is particularly interesting because it contains incised sherds identical in decorative technique and motif to those of the late Machalilla Phase, as well as zoned red painting, a Chorrera Phase diagnostic. It is significant that this evidence comes from an area connected

Fig. 13

to the Guayas basin by the Yaguachi river drainage, a rela-

TRAIT	MACHALILLA PHASE	OCÓS PHASE	CHORRERA PHASE
Cylindrical spout	×		×
Stirrup spout	×		×
Carinated (angular) bowl	×		×
Fine incision (Ayangue Incised)	×		×
Red banding	×		×
Double-line incision	×		×
Nicked shoulder embellishment	×		×
Simple burnished-line decoration	?	×	×
Rocker stamping		×	×
Iridescent painting		×	×
Dentate stamping		×	×
Everted-rim bowl		×	×
Undulating or lobed rim		×	×
Incision bordering rim on interior		×	×
Pottery whistle		×	×
Obsidian chips and flakes		×	×
Zoned red and black			×
Annular base			×
Napkin-ring ear spool			×

Fig. 17. *Traits linking the Chorrera Phase with the Machalilla Phase and with the Ocós Phase of coastal Guatemala*

tively easy natural route followed today by the Guayaquil–
Quito railroad.

Farther to the south-east, at Cerro Narrío near Cañar, a
much larger sherd sample is available that includes the types
represented in the Alausí region, plus lobed-rim bowls, annular bases, and iridescent painting. The fact that the motifs of
incised designs in both places resemble most closely those of the
Machalilla Phase, while the vessel shapes to which they are
applied are more like those of the Chorrera Phase, suggests that
the influence may date from near the time of transition. Additional support for this hypothesis is provided by two stirrup-
spout jars, one from Descanso in the Cuenca basin, and the
other from Loja. Both are clearly intermediate between the
Machalilla Phase spout form and that associated with the Kotosh Period at Kotosh in the central Peruvian highlands, which
marks the earliest dated occurrence of the stirrup spout in Peru.

Plate 17

Although few in number, these ceramic traits are distinctive
enough to suggest that coastal agriculturalists exercised strong
influence in the southern highlands at the beginning of the
Late Formative Period. Probably, maize was introduced at this
time, since the Alausí basin in particular is well suited to its
cultivation. For ease of reference pending discovery of sites that
will permit more detailed description, this complex has been
tentatively designated here as the Alausí Phase.

Other potsherds from Alausí represent a different ceramic
tradition. Among the decorative elements are zones of punctation bounded by incision, broad incision filled with red or
white inlay subsequent to firing, and rows of single or concentric rings. All are characteristic of the earliest pottery complexes at Kotosh, Peru, which in the preceding chapter were
viewed as the result of a southern diffusion of pottery-making
through the highlands during the Early Formative Period.
Unfortunately, the sherds from Alausí are out of context and
undated, making it uncertain whether they belong to this earlier

period or whether they constitute survivals amalgamated into the ceramic complex of the Alausí Phase.

So far, nothing resembling the pottery of the coastal Late Formative has been reported north of the Cuenca-Alausí region. This may reflect the state of archaeological investigation rather than the true situation. However, it is also possible that the more extreme environmental conditions of the arid Ambato-Riobamba basin or the pre-existence of an established ceramic tradition inhibited the northward diffusion of the Chorrera-Machalilla Phase influences.

ECOLOGICAL FACTORS AND THE END OF THE FORMATIVE PERIOD

The relatively rapid spread of the Chorrera Phase over much of the coast and into the southern highlands is an indication of its generalized nature and relatively great flexibility and adaptability. Maintenance of its sociopolitical organization did not depend upon large numbers or concentrations of people, and its subsistence technology was not specialized toward particular environmental conditions. However, with the passage of centuries, territorial boundaries became established, population increased and knowledge of the special qualities of local environments improved. Seasonal vagaries became better understood, and annual variations in rainfall could be partly compensated for with broadened experience. Regional differences in frequency and severity of drought years set limitations of varying latitude and intensity on crop yield per man hour of labour and on the possibility of accumulating surpluses for sustenance of non-food-producers or for security against years of lean harvest. Such environmental factors and technological adjustments underlie differences in population density, which in turn affect the complexity of sociopolitical and religious organization, commerce and many other aspects of culture.

Added to environmental forces tending to channel cultural development in ways that can be recognized as adaptive is the process of cultural drift, which makes some degree of change an inevitable correlate of time. Instability is the natural condition of the universe and the appearance of stability is a reflection of the brief perspective of the viewer or of the effectiveness of stabilizing selection. Thus, when two groups of common ancestry are prevented from close interaction, they will tend to differentiate culturally and linguistically even without external pressures for change. About 500 BC the combined action of such factors resulted in the emergence of a number of distinct regional cultures in Ecuador.

CHAPTER V

The Regional Developmental Period

GENERAL CHARACTERISTICS

THE REGIONAL DEVELOPMENTAL PERIOD is the time of differentiation in sociopolitical organization, florescence in art style and elaboration in technology. Pottery container forms proliferate into goblets, compoteras (shallow bowls on a tall, wide pedestal base), polypod and tetrapod bowls with a variety of leg shapes. Decorative techniques are more diverse than during any other period. Pottery becomes a medium for production of numerous kinds of small artifacts, in addition to an abundance of figurines, which are often mould-made. Dress and ornament include elaborate costumes and head-dresses, executed in textiles and feathers. Bracelets, neck-laces and anklets depicted on figurines have parallels in beads, pendants and miscellaneous trinkets carved from shell and stone. For the first time there is direct evidence of metallurgy.

Few cemeteries of this period have been scientifically exca-vated, so that evidence comes principally from broken artifacts discarded in village refuse. What can be recovered archaeologic-ally, however, will always be a small fraction of what once must have existed, since no direct evidence remains of wood-carving, basketry, textiles or other perishable objects. These factors make the cultural level on the Ecuadorian coast seem considerably simpler than that on the contemporary coast of Peru, a contrast that might be diminished if conditions of pre-servation in the two regions were more alike.

Although varying widely in degree of elaboration, the Regional Developmental Period archaeological phases share elements that serve as horizon markers. Outstanding in pottery decoration are white painting on a red-slipped or plain surface and negative painting on a plain, red-slipped or white-slipped surface. The latter technique is so named because it consists of application after firing of a resistant material to the vessel surface in the pattern of the desired design. The vessel is then dipped in an organic solution, for example a mixture of soot and honey, which clings to the unprotected zones. Reheating in a reducing atmosphere fixes the organic paint so that when the resistant material is removed the design appears in the negative. In some local styles, white and negative paint are combined either on a plain surface or a red slip, while in others red stripes or solid areas accent negative designs. In a few regions, negative painting is rare and polychrome designs are executed in black and red on a buff or white-slipped surface before firing or in multiple colours applied after firing.

Fig. 18

Pottery of the Regional Developmental Period is characterized by multiplication of vessel shapes. The low ring base of Chorrera Phase bowls diversifies into short and tall pedestal bases, sometimes closed at the bottom to create a rattle by insertion of loose pellets. Polypod, tetrapod and tripod bowls exhibit a wide variety of leg form; these are solid or hollow, conical, cylindrical, mammiform or U-shaped, and may be painted, modelled, appliqué-decorated or plain. Jars typically have globular bodies and strongly everted rims, although angular-shouldered forms are popular in some regions.

Aside from ceramic modifications, the most typical feature of the Regional Developmental Period is proliferation of what might be called minor art objects. In addition to figurines, whistles in the shape of birds, animals or shells, stools, masks, flat and roller stamps made of pottery, and beads, pendants and *atlatl* (spear-thrower) hooks carved of shell or stone have been reported from all but poorly known regions. Head-rests, pipes and house models are more limited in distribution. It is probable that similar artistry was applied to bone and wood, while figurine treatment indicates that textiles and featherwork were highly elaborated.

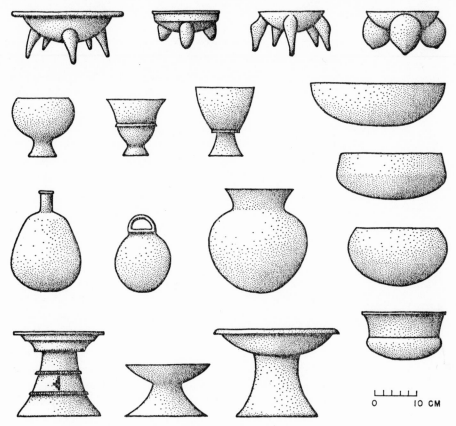

Fig. 18. Diagnostic vessel shapes of the Regional Developmental Period

In characterizing the Regional Developmental Period as one of general technological and artistic florescence, it is necessary to recognize that not all regions attained an equal level of complexity. On the coast, the Jama-Coaque and Tolita Phases of northern Manabí and Esmeraldas far outstripped the Jambelí Phase of El Oro and the Tejar Phase of the Guayas Basin. Contemporary highland phases are poorly known but what can be deduced suggests an intermediate status. Several factors account for this inequality, but two are particularly important:

(1) differences in the environments, presenting varying poten-
tials for exploitation and varying difficulties in realizing this
potential, (2) differential accessibility to outside influences
bringing new art styles, religious cults and technological innovations from near or distant regions. It is during this period
that the diversity of Ecuadorian geography and the multi-
plicity of natural land and water routes most obviously exert
their influence.

Fig. 19
Eight generally contemporary archaeological phases represent
the Regional Developmental Period on the coast. Two more
have been tentatively recognized in the southern highlands on
the basis of published data, and these attest the presence of
diagnostic coastal horizon markers. The remainder of the highlands has not as yet produced any remains clearly assignable
to the Regional Developmental Period.

THE GUANGALA PHASE

The coastal segment between southern Manabí, approximately
in the latitude of La Plata Island, and the modern village of
Chanduy abounds in sites of the Guangala Phase. The only
detailed description is by G. H. S. Bushnell, who conducted
excavations at Guangala and La Libertad. Evidence of habitation occurs both adjacent to the shore and inland on the banks
of rivers flowing from the Colonche Hills. A dispersed settlement pattern appears to be reflected in these small shallow sites,
which probably represent hamlets scattered over the more fertile
portions of the landscape. Clay with twig impressions indicates that houses were of wattle-and-daub construction, probably with thatched roofs.

The strongest evidence of the importance of maize agriculture
comes from the abundance of *mano* and *metate* fragments at all
Guangala Phase sites. The *mano*, or hand-held stone, is a long
cylinder that extends beyond the sides of the grinding-slab, or

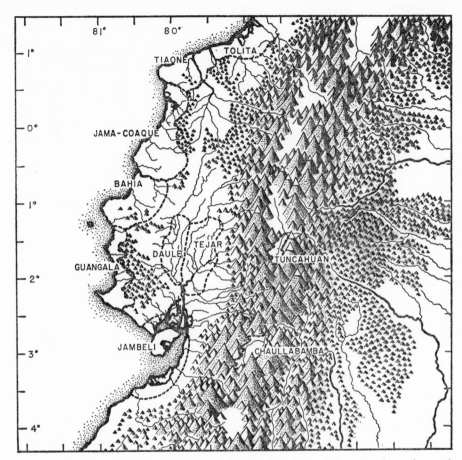

Fig. 19. Geographical distribution of the various archaeological phases of the Regional Developmental Period. Mountains cover areas above the 300 metre contour

metate. As one surface is worn by use, a broad shallow U-shaped groove develops, ultimately weakening the back of the *mano* to the point of fracture. Pottery bowls with deeply incised interiors must have served as graters to judge from the wear that they show, and it has been suggested that sweet manioc or pep-

71

Ecuador

Fig. 24b

pers were pulped in them. Small shell boxes containing white powder reflect the practice of chewing coca with lime.

In addition to farming, shell-fish and fish continued to be exploited by the shore villagers, and deer were hunted in the interior. Continuity with the Early Formative can be observed in reamers and sandstone saws for working shell, but the fish-hook has changed its form from circular to a nearly straight shank with an in-curved hook. One or two small projections at the back of the shank indicate a modification in manner of attachment of the line. Small stones and pieces of ground shell encircled with a groove served as net or line weights. The appearance of shell *atlatl* hooks implies the use of this weapon, but projectiles are unrepresented with the possible exception of sting-ray spines modified for hafting, which Bushnell suggests may have served as dart points.

Polished celts and chisels of stone or shell attest to the working of wood, although no examples of the products survive. Lamellar obsidian flakes show only use retouch, and carefully chipped stone tools are not characteristic. Bone awls and copper needles complete the tool-kit, aside from cobbles and flakes used for chopping, hammering and miscellaneous cutting, drilling and grinding operations.

Beads and simple pendants of cut and polished shell, biconically perforated stone beads, shell nose-rings, and whole shells perforated for suspension were used for personal ornament. Figurines, although unrealistic in comparison to those of the Bahía and Jama-Coaque Phases, have incised and painted decoration that may represent face and body painting. Clothing is seldom shown, but one type wears a broad collar and another a short straight skirt. Nose-rings as well as ear ornaments or perforations of the lobe for their insertion are typical. The most frequent ornament is one circular pellet in the lobe with another above. Other figurines show a ring through the lobe with a second hanging from it. Artificial deformation of the skull, in

Fig. 20

the form of occipital flattening, continues a practice introduced to this portion of the coast by the Machalilla Phase.

A number of metal objects have been reported from the Guangala Phase area, but most are surface finds that may be of later date. Several kinds, however, are clearly of Guangala Phase manufacture. Hammering appears to be the only technique employed. Copper needles have the eye formed by flattening one end into a disk, perforating the centre and folding the sides together leaving a slit opposite the perforation, a technique distinct from that employed in the later Milagro Phase. Copper fish-hooks have small projections at the upper rear of the shank paralleling the form of the shell hooks. The only known copper ornament is a thin flat nose-ring. Small five-pointed stars (also produced in pottery) and narrow spatulas served unknown functions.

Disposal of the dead took place in the village, perhaps beneath the house floor. Bushnell has described two types of burial: extended primary and secondary. Some individuals had grave goods, others did not. Besides pottery vessels, the following objects were represented: fish-hook reamer, grooved stone net or line weight, polished stone celt, shell fish-hook, shell pendant, shell figurine, bone awl, conch shell box, copper needle, copper fish-hook. Offerings appear to be correlated with the sex of the deceased, but provide no clear evidence of difference in status or rank.

Of possible religious significance are pottery figurines. Less abundant and simpler than those of the contemporary cultures to the north, they run the gamut from extreme stylization to realism. The smallest and most unrealistic Guangala Phase figurines are flat rectanguloid bars of clay, slightly expanding at the head and bifurcated at the opposite end into two stubby legs. The front of the torso is covered with incision, sharply defined but somewhat haphazardly drawn with a pointed tool in vertical, zigzag or zoned patterns of straight lines. The sex may

Fig. 20a

73

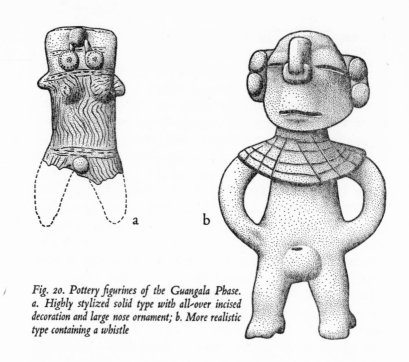

Fig. 20. Pottery figurines of the Guangala Phase. a. Highly stylized solid type with all-over incised decoration and large nose ornament; b. More realistic type containing a whistle

Fig. 20b

be male, female or undefined. The height is typically less than 12 cm.

A more common and standardized type is a sexless or possibly male figure, nude except for a wide collar extending from the neck down over the shoulders. Eyes and mouth are horizontal slits, while the nose is in high relief and usually decorated with a heavy ring hanging from the septum. The ears stand out prominently and are nearly covered by two large circular studs or buttons, one above the other. The arms curve from shoulder to hip and hands are not differentiated. Legs are separated and slightly expanded forward and backward to produce feet with concave soles. The body contains a whistle in the pubic region. The surface is smoothed and sometimes polished and negative-painted or red-slipped. Height averages around 16 cm.

One type is mould-made, probably influenced by the com- Plate 23
mon technique of groups farther to the north, with which
stylistic resemblances can also be detected. The face is realistic,
with almond eyes, curved mouth, slightly bulbous nose with
perforated septum, rounded cheeks and well-defined chin.
Male examples are standing, with arms at the sides or bent
toward the front and holding a child. Female examples are
usually kneeling with hands resting on thighs, and are clothed
in a short skirt. The surface is well smoothed and polished to
high lustre. Torso, arms and legs are decorated with geometric
figures in paired or triple incisions sometimes with the addition
of red or negative painting. Standing examples are 20 to 30 cm.
tall.

In addition to figurines incorporating whistles, pottery
whistles take the form of small bird-like creatures or roly-poly
dogs with up-curved tail. Tubular pottery flutes assume at-
tenuated anthropomorphic forms or terminate in a bird. Deer-
bone flutes also occur.

Guangala Phase pottery stamps are characteristically long,
narrow rectangles with a conical projection at the centre back
for grasping. The pattern on the slightly convex face is a fine
checkerboard of incised and excised diamonds or squares, or
more rarely zigzag lines paralleling the long axis. The stamp
face is 8 to 11 cm. long by 1·8 to 2·8 cm. wide. Roller stamps
are rare.

Another ceramic artifact is the spindle whorl. Perforated
sherd disks may have served this function, but bead-like examples, often with turreted tops are more common. Such
whorls are usually decorated with incision or zoned punctation.
In conjunction with copper needles, their presence suggests a
textile industry whose only direct evidence is fabric impressions
left on the interior of mould-made figurines.

Pottery shows technological advance over that of the preceding period in better control of firing. Buff and black wares

are consistently produced by regulating the presence of oxygen during firing, while a red ware was obtained through appli/cation of a slip. Fine compact paste and walls 2 to 5 mm. thick are characteristic of rounded and slightly carinated bowls, while thicker walls and more sandy paste are typical of larger vessels. A dichotomy between pottery types of obviously utili/tarian function and those more delicately formed and tastefully decorated culminates a trend evident in Chorrera Phase pottery. Although overshadowed by new vessel shapes and new decorative techniques, many Guangala Phase pottery types are traceable to Chorrera Phase antecedents. Among the survivals are iridescent painting and application of red slip to the lip and rim interior of plain jars.

In addition to white/on/red and negative painting, which are shared with other ceramic complexes of the Regional Developmental Period, several decorative techniques charac/terize the Guangala Phase. One of the most striking is poly/chrome painting in bright red/orange and black on the buff/coloured exterior walls of rounded or slightly carinated bowls. Solid stripes at the rim and at the waist define a band in which a wide variety of motifs are executed, either in continuation or in a series of rectangular panels. Black rectilinear strokes out/line areas filled either with solid red or with a row of black dots. Except for slightly to markedly stylized bird forms, motifs are geometrical and predominantly rectilinear. Equally attractive are bowls with red/on/buff painting incorporating some of the polychrome motifs but making greater use of vertical or diagonal parallel lines and continuing patterns, without subdivision into discrete panels.

Plate 21

Plate 19

Decoration by burnished lines on an unpolished surface is another typical Guangala Phase technique, applied principally to the interior of open bowls with a depression at the centre sur/rounding a small perforation. The walls are polished black, while the unpolished interior is grey. Burnished zones contain

Fig. 21. Conical legs from Guangala Phase polypod bowls with anthropomorphic decoration by appliqué

Fig. 21

standardized motifs: a band of parallel strokes or diagonal hachure along the outer edge and a band of curlicues along the inner edge. Additional design elements include concentric semicircles and a vertical line crossed by horizontal lines of graduated lengths. Other characteristic decorative techniques are finger painting in simple parallel bands, and narrow closely spaced stripes covering the surface. Appliqué is utilized for converting solid polypod legs into human caricatures, often with sorrowful expressions.

In addition to globular jars with everted rims and rounded bowls, Guangala Phase vessels assume a variety of slightly angular to markedly shouldered forms. Bases may be rounded, annular, pedestal or polypod; polypod legs occur in conical or cylindrical forms and may be solid or hollow. Rounded or flaring-walled goblets have short pedestals that frequently are enclosed to create a rattle. Compoteras are often decorated with white-on-red painting. Bottles are rare. All vessel shapes and decorated as well as undecorated pottery types occur in village refuse, implying that whatever specialized functions they may have served were part of village life.

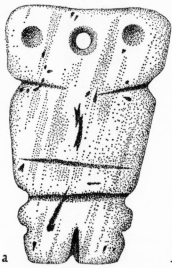

Fig. 22. *Shell objects from the Jambelí Phase.*
a. Anthropomorphic pendant; b, c. Side and
a   *front views of a bird*

Although the Guangala Phase is distinct in nearly all respects from the Bahía Phase, its neighbour to the north, evidence
of contact between the two exists in the form of trade objects,
such as a Bahía Phase anthropomorphic tusk-like ornament
from the Santa Elena Peninsula. Cylindrical or roller stamps,
which are rare and typically differ in design pattern from the
flat Guangala type, may be trade items also. The close similarity in surface finish, decorative technique and motif, and
vessel shape between Guangala White-on-Red and Jambelí
White-on-Red suggests that the technique and perhaps some
of the vessels may have been acquired from the Jambelí Phase.

THE JAMBELÍ PHASE

Plate 5

Around the mouth of the Rio Guayas and extending across the
Peruvian frontier, the coast is fringed by mangrove. West of the
Guayas, salitres are gradually replacing the swamp, while in El

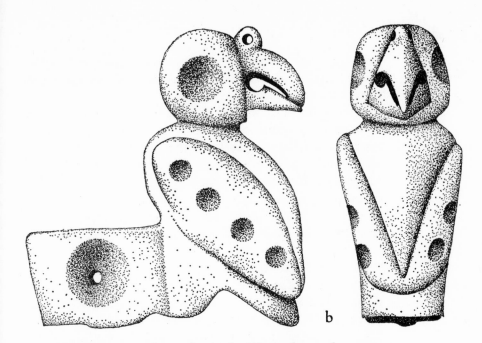

b

Oro the process is less advanced. Throughout the area, including the island of Puná, small shell middens occur on unflooded land bordering inlets, rivers and swamps. Many contain pottery, chips and fireburnt rocks. Refuse covers a small area and accumulation rarely exceeds 50 cm. in thickness. While the principal subsistence resource probably was the sea, shell *atlatl* hooks imply that hunting was practised. *Manos* and *metates* were used for the preparation of plant foods.

Artifacts of stone and shell are rare. Although no shell fishhooks have been found, their existence is implied by sandstone saws. Hammer/stones are natural cobbles pitted or chipped from use. Skills not illustrated in the manufacture of tools are reflected in well/shaped and polished circular beads of basalt, shale, serpentine and chlorite schist. Similar beads of spondylus shell are often attractively two/toned, partly red or orange and partly white. Simple cut shell pendants with one or two perforations, or small complete shells perforated at one end for suspension are most common, but occasional anthropomorphic examples occur. A beautifully carved bird with its head turned toward the rear exhibits rare realism.

Perhaps the most unusual Jambelí Phase artifact is a stone bark beater, so identified on the basis of similarity to beaters used for manufacturing bark cloth in Mesoamerica. It is a flat rectanguloid stone with straight or slightly convex sides and rounded corners. Paralleling the long axis on one face are three to four deep grooves, somewhat unevenly spaced. No spindle whorls have been reported with the possible exception of tur-reted bead-like examples of soft stone and several perforated sherd disks.

Fig. 23

Jambelí Phase figurines represent a distinctive, highly stylized type. The body is hollow, slightly expanding in diameter below the neck and then tapering to a single foot open at the bottom. Short incisions on the upper front of the foot suggest toes. Arms are stubby projections at the shoulder, some-times nicked to represent fingers. Heads are characteristically about twice as broad as they are high, rounded in profile coming to a ridge along the top. The eyes are the most variable feature, but a diamond executed by four short incisions with a punctation in the middle is most common. Ornamentation is by incision and painting. Horizontal incised lines across the top of the head are often interspersed with vertical cuts or nicks defining zones painted white or red. Apart from fingers and toes, the body is rarely incised. The front half is typically well smoothed, after which some examples were red slipped and negative or white painted. Most examples are fragmentary, but two complete figurines suggest a size range between about 6 and 16 cm.

Jambelí Phase pottery does not reach the technological com-petence of the best Guangala Phase wares. There is also less variety in decoration. White-on-red and negative-on-red, the only painted techniques employed, are used independently or in

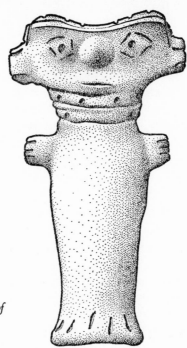

Fig. 23. Typical hollow pottery figurine of the Jambelí Phase

combination. In addition to simple patterns painted in white on a red-slipped surface, white and red are applied in adjacent zones. Negative designs feature narrow stripes and bands filled with dots. Red bands ornament the vessel lip or occur concentrically on bowl interiors. Unslipped exteriors of pedestals or of compotera flanges bear incision in simple rectilinear patterns of stepped and parallel lines, often defining fields containing a ring-and-dot or a small triangular or circular perforation. Small appliqué bird and animal heads are rare.

In addition to shallow bowls with direct, expanded, everted or interiorly thickened rims and globular, everted-rim jars, there are several specialized vessel shapes. One is a globular jar with a heavy exteriorly thickened rim. Another is a large compotera with a wide skirt-like flange projecting downward along the outer edge of the rim. Hollow and solid polypods occur, as well as tall and low annular bases. Spouts represent bottles, some with handles.

Scattered throughout the Jambelí Phase are indications of Guangala Phase contact. Most abundant are sherds of distinc- tive Guangala Phase decorated pottery types, including striped painting, finger painting and iridescent painting. Several arti- facts resemble common Guangala Phase objects, but differ sufficiently to suggest that they may be local copies rather than traded pieces. One is a shell box, larger and more carefully carved than those of the Guangala Phase ; another is a figurine body fragment with a broad collar and arms curved from shoulder to hip generally resembling one of the most popular Guangala Phase types. The stone bark beaters and an unusual figurine head with characteristics reminiscent of La Plata Seated examples reflect contact with the more distant Bahía Phase on the southern Manabí coast.

Fig. 24a

THE TEJAR AND DAULE PHASES

Along the banks of the rivers draining the Guayas basin, numerous small habitation sites imply a way of life not mark- edly different from that on the ocean shore. Accumulations of refuse up to about two metres in thickness reflect a considerable degree of permanency of residence, particularly since bulky shell remains are not a component. A pottery vessel from the Río Babahoyo shows a nearly square house having a double-sloped roof with a high straight ridge and slightly overhanging eaves.

Plate 20

Fish were undoubtedly taken from the rivers, but the un- availability of other kinds of seafood was more than compen- sated by the greater productivity of farming. Although neither *atlatl* hooks nor *manos* and *metates* have been reported, this probably reflects the relatively slight amount of archaeological investigation in this region rather than a real difference in sub- sistence pattern or food preparation. Pottery grater bowls

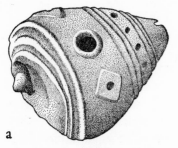
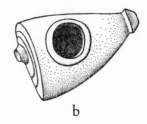

a

b

Fig. 24. Whole shells with a perforation for use as a container, possibly for lime. a. Jambelí Phase; b. Guangala Phase

occur, the interior deeply incised with straight lines radiating from the centre. In some instances, the slightly raised rim is broken by a channel for drainage.

Stone implements are limited to flakes of obsidian, quartzite and chalcedony, hammer-stones, polishing stones and a few polished adzes and axes. Shell, the principal raw material for the manufacture of beads, pendants and other small objects on the coast, is unavailable locally and was not obtained by trade. Flat disk-shaped stone beads are rare. Except for awls, bone artifacts have not been reported. A unique kind of object is a small pebble sometimes dyed red over the whole surface, but more typically on both ends leaving an undyed band 4 to 9 mm. wide around the middle. Either natural water-worn stones or crudely shaped fragments were dyed. Length ranges from 2 to 4 cm.

A number of pottery artifacts occur, including plain bead-like spindle whorls and perforated sherd disks that may have served the same purpose. Tubular flutes with anthropomorphic ornamentation are relatively common. Flat stamps, rectanguloid in outline, are rare. Two small linked copper rings are the only evidence of metallurgy.

Figurine body fragments are scattered in the refuse, but most heads are surface finds or undocumented as to provenance. However, the Mate type (see p. 59) is represented at a sufficient

Fig. 15c

number of sites to suggest that it can be attributed to the Tejar Phase, although it may have originated in the preceding Chorrera Phase. Larger hollow heads are beautifully sculptured and wear helmets carved in asymmetrical patterns of raised and depressed zones, which may be painted green, orange, red and white. The face is sometimes white-slipped.

The pottery of the Daule and Tejar Phases resembles that of the Jambelí Phase in emphasis on white-on-red and negative-painted decoration, while sharing with the Guangala Phase such vessel shapes as rattle-based goblets and angular-shouldered bowls. Tripod and polypod bowls are rare. Negative painting occurs principally on compoteras and goblets, and all combinations are represented: negative zones bordered by red bands, adjoining red and white-slipped zones both negative-painted, negative and white painting on a red-slipped background, negative on a red-painted and white-slipped surface, and negative on polished red or polished white slip. Small or large dots and narrow to wide bands are the most common elements, from which a variety of designs are produced. White-on-red patterns also typically consist of bands and rows of dots. If one technique can be said to be diagnostic of this region, however, it is the execution of zoned designs on unpolished surfaces with incision defining bands or triangular or stepped areas alternately filled with punctation and painted red.

Bottles, characteristic of the antecedent Chorrera Phase, appear to have maintained greater popularity here than on other parts of the coast. A strap handle frequently rises along the inner edge and loops around to terminate in a bird-head containing a whistle. Square or rectangular outline is frequent. One example

Fig. 25

has two turrets, one with a spout and the other with a bird containing a whistle, linked by a bridge handle. The broken edge left at the base of the spout has been smoothed over, indicating that the vessel continued in use after it was damaged. Iridescent painting decorates the sides.

Fig. 25. Rectanguloid vessel from the Tejar Phase with iridescent-painted bands and spots (hachure) on the sides. The bird contains a whistle. The other turret had a spout, which was broken off in antiquity

Evidence of contact with contemporary phases in adjacent regions is reflected in the presence of sherds of 'foreign' pottery types. Most common are fragments of Bahía Polychrome, originating on the southern Manabí coast. Guangala Burnished-line bowls and anthropomorphic polypod legs also occur. Mate-type figurine heads have been reported from Guangala, Bahía and Tolita Phase sites, but absence of reliable information as to source makes it impossible to distinguish traded examples from possible copies. Such contacts do not appear to have led to any significant amount of acculturation on the part of the Guayas basin people, and evidence of religious developments comparable to those on the Manabí and Esmeraldas coasts during the Regional Developmental Period is absent.

THE BAHÍA PHASE

Plate 2

The Ecuadorian coast from the latitude of La Plata Island northward to the Bahía de Caráquez is the most heavily populated littoral zone in modern times. Here are located the towns of Manta, Portoviejo, Jipijapa and Bahía, along with many smaller settlements. Some were founded in the colonial period, while others overlie aboriginal towns. Although the best-known Bahía Phase sites have been destroyed or are in the process of engulfment by expanding city limits, enough information has been salvaged to indicate that this area was characterized during the Regional Developmental Period by greater urbanism, more highly developed sociopolitical organization and more elaborate religious practices than contemporary culture areas to the south and in the interior.

Bahía Phase sites are characterized by the presence of platform mounds in addition to accumulations of habitation refuse. When Jijón y Caamaño visited Manta in 1923, he noted that it was 'full of mounds', all of which have since been destroyed. Some had the sides stepped in three or four terraces held in place by walls of uncut stones. Access to the summit was provided by ramps or a staircase at one end. A group of similar platforms without stone retaining walls was mapped by Estrada in 1960 in the eastern suburb of Manta known as Esteros. These mounds were principally rectangular in outline, 50 to 175 metres long by 20 to 50 metres wide, with no consistent orientation. Scattered among them were seven depressions believed by Estrada to have served as reservoirs.

The existence of a number of pottery house models aids reconstruction of the Bahía Phase house type, which is sharply divergent from the simple style associated with the Tejar Phase. The most universal characteristic is curvature of the ridge, with the front and rear gables often rising to a height double that from the ground to the centre of the ridge. In addition to this saddle roof construction, the ridge often projects slightly out/ ward over the front and rear walls. In most instances, there is some kind of embellishment. Two examples have a double roof, with a hollow zone between the upper and lower ridges. Another has a slightly concave ridge onto which large orna/ mental projections are set near the front and back. These and additional ornaments near the eaves are covered with appliqué fillets and pellets. Several houses have narrow appliqué strips laid crosswise on the ridge.

Walls are vertical and the only opening is usually at the front, although a few models show a rear door also. Sometimes the entire front is left open except for a band at the top following the slope of the gable, while other houses have a rectangular entrance. In two instances, a circular column just inside the doorway supports the ridge pole. Several examples retain traces of painted decoration in red, yellow, green and black on the walls. A human figure is sometimes seated in the doorway. Although some are containers, many are simply models. This non/utilitarian nature suggests a ceremonial function, perhaps as a small household shrine.

Stone implements of the Bahía Phase are comparable to those of the rest of the coast in lack of consistent form, with the ex/ ception of bark beaters of the type already described for the Jambelí Phase. Shell beads, pendants, and fish/hooks, and bone awls and punches are common. A flat gold nose/ring is evidence of the use of metal.

The Bahía Phase differs from other Regional Developmental Period cultures in the presence of several types of carved stone objects without clearly recognizable function. Best known are small blocks cut from greyish/white volcanic tuff. Square ex/ amples are between 10 and 13 cm. square by 6 to 9 cm. thick, while circular ones are 11 to 14 cm. in diameter by 5 to 8 cm. thick. With rare exceptions, only one face is decorated by cleanly cut incisions and rings, the latter produced by rotation of

Fig. 26a

a hollow cane. The pattern consists of diagonal bands of even width or tapering from the centre toward the corners.

Speculation on the possible function of these blocks is rendered difficult by two considerations: (1) undecorated examples of both circular and square varieties occur, and (2) finds have been restricted to La Plata Island, which other evidence indicates to have been a ceremonial centre. Dorsey, who collected the majority of the specimens, considered and rejected the theory that they were used in a game because of inconsistency in number and placement of the rings. Estrada suggested that they served as navigation aids, an explanation that does not seem to account for their absence from mainland sites, or for the numerous unincised examples. Interpretation of the blocks *Fig. 26b* should take into account smaller rectangular stones with square cross-section, which also occur in two forms: either undecorated or decorated with a row of rings with central dots on two opposite faces or on all four faces. Some are perforated lengthwise, Length ranges from 4 to 9 cm., thickness from 2·0 to 2·7 cm. These are also reported only from La Plata Island.

Fig. 26. Bahía Phase carved stone blocks from La Plata Island. a. Square block with decoration on one face; b. Rectangular 'bead' with ring-and-dot ornamentation on two sides

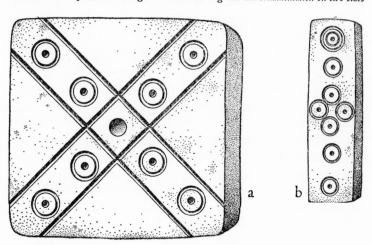

a   b

Another unique type of object is an amulet with anthro-pomorphic features incised either on the inner side of a slightly curved tusk-like stone or on a flat slab of rectanguloid or asym-metrical outline. Examples have been found both on the island of La Plata and in habitation sites on the mainland. The tusk-shaped form has a face with an ovoid eye and mouth and a parallel-sided nose. Horizontal cuts suggest hands. Flat plaques, by contrast, usually have the eyes and mouth in the form of small rectangles, a triangular nose, and long, slender arms. Some of both kinds are notched at the sides or perforated horizontally near the upper end, apparently for suspension, in spite of their weight. Similarly shaped pendants are worn by some of the figurines, especially the La Plata Seated type.

Pottery artifacts are abundant. Flat stamps are intermediate in complexity of patterning between those of the Guangala Phase to the south and the Jama-Coaque Phase to the north, and a few of the cylindrical variety also occur. Whistles are modelled in bird and animal forms, in addition to being embedded in some types of figurines. Rectanguloid plaques with two per-forations near each end, modelled from clay or carved from sherds, may have served as net weights. One has decoration in the ring-and-dot motif characteristic of the stone blocks. Rec-tanguloid objects with upturned sides and four small feet have been identified as models of cradles, although none have oc-cupants. Small golf-tee-shaped ear plugs have a shallow to deeply concave expanded end, sometimes bearing traces of post-fired painting or red wash.

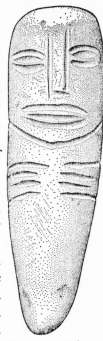

Fig. 27. Tusk-shaped stone with anthropomorphic carving on the interior face. Bahía Phase

Perhaps the most unusual pottery artifacts are neck- or head-rests, so identified on the basis of similarity to head-rests still in use in parts of Asia, Oceania and Africa. A flat rectanguloid slab forming the base is connected to a slightly concave upper slab of similar size by various kinds of supports, including a single pillar, two or three circular columns, and a pair of out-ward-facing caryatid figures. A less common type has solid walls. The majority are about 15 cm. long and 8 to 10 cm. high at the centre. Many head‑rests are red‑slipped and polished, others are polished and decorated by incision on the concave upper surface. Anthropomorphic examples characteristically wear the wide bracelets and have other details connecting them with La Plata Seated figurines.

Plate 40

Figurines of the Bahía Phase are numerous and varied. Many are completely mould‑made, while others have mould‑made faces and hand‑modelled bodies. Pottery moulds of both kinds supplement evidence from the figurines themselves. Figurines modelled completely by hand are also abundant.

Bahía Phase figurines are of interest not only because of the ritual practices they reflect, but because of the information they can provide on dress and ornament. Bahía, La Plata Hollow and La Plata Solid types are typically post‑fired painted in geometric patterns, but in most cases it is not clear whether these are to be interpreted as body painting or painted cloth. Female figurines often wear a short straight skirt, leaving the upper

Fig. 28. Profile and front view of a small solid Estero type figurine of the Bahía Phase

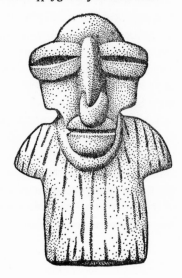

Fig. 29. Mould-made figurine of the Bahía type, often decorated with post-fired painting

body bare. The bodies of the highly stylized Estero type are Fig. 28
covered with rows of short incisions in a variety of patterns, the
interpretation of which is dubious.

Ornamentation is realistically portrayed. Necklaces take the
form of a single strand of ovoid or discoidal beads, or a simple
single or double band with or without a tusk-like pendant at
the centre front. Bracelets and anklets are usually plain bands,
but more elaborate variations include a row of conical studs,
beads, perforated circular pellets, punctated bands, and bands
with small cup-like prominences. This ornament may occur
just below the knee as well as at the ankle. Nose-rings, which
are almost universal, are thickest at the centre and taper toward the ends, which are inserted into the septum. Bahía-type Fig. 29
figurines have a perforation in the septum for insertion of such a
ring. Ear ornamentation is variable, but most patterns employ
small circular studs. A single stud may be inserted in the lobe,
or a row may follow the margin of the ear. A few figurines wear
a cup-like ornament that resembles the pottery 'golf-tee'

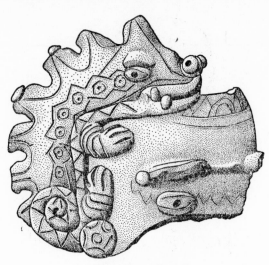

Fig. 30. Portion of a Bahía Phase anthropomorphic figurine from La Plata Island with a 'dragon' head-dress

Plate 26

Fig. 30

examples abundant in all sites. Less typical is a hollow ring inserted in the lobe, or a dangling ring. Lip ornaments are rare.

Elaborate head-dress is restricted to La Plata Seated figurines, which exhibit a variety of helmet-like styles, some with conical studs over the entire surface, others with flaps extending downward at the sides. A bonnet-like version has a broad brim projecting forward across the top and down both sides, which may be plain, painted and incised, or more ornately fashioned into dragon-like creatures.

Religion appears to have focused on a sanctuary on La Plata Island, to which pilgrimages may have been made. Dorsey, who investigated the island at the beginning of this century, found no evidence of habitation. The best bay is near the centre of the eastern side. Here, at the head of a ravine leading down from the summit, Dorsey found concentrated refuse composed almost entirely of figurine fragments, decorated and plain stone blocks, stone beads (including turquoise), and three tusk-shaped stones with anthropomorphic carving. He estimated the fragments to represent about a thousand figurines and perhaps twelve vessels. Most were crudely finished compared to main-

Fig. 31. Bahía Phase bottle with three globular chambers, two surmounted by human figures and the third by a spout. A handle bridges the centre. The figures wear a bonnet-like head-dress and a necklace with a tusk-shaped pendant, and hold a snake in each hand. They are painted after firing with white, green, yellow, black and red. The chamber with the spout is polished and iridescent-painted

land examples and only half a dozen showed any trace of painting.

Bahía Phase religion seems to have featured serpents and dragon-like elements. A tripartite bottle is surmounted by two impressive figures holding a snake in each hand. Their head-dresses and the tusk-like pendant on their necklaces relates them to the La Plata Seated figurines, one of which has a snake coiled around each arm. This configuration plus the realism and individuality of facial modelling suggests that the La Plata Seated figurines may depict priests in acts of prayer. If so, the characteristic leg position, in which one leg rests on top of the other, probably has ceremonical significance as it does throughout Asia.

Fig. 31

Plate 26

This resemblance in sitting position between Asian and Bahía Phase images might be dismissed as coincidence were it not for the presence of other Asiatic elements in the material culture of the Bahía Phase, such as head-rests and saddle-roofed house models. Another Asiatic feature represented on a number of figurines is a Pan-pipe with tubes graduated toward the centre rather than from one side to the other in typical New World fashion. The tusk-like pendants and 'golf-tee' ear plugs also have Asiatic prototypes. Since all of these traits are not only widely distributed in the Old World, but of greater antiquity there than they are on the Ecuadorian coast, their appearance in the Bahía Phase is best explained as the result of transpacific contact.

Although this drifting craft would have been propelled by the same combination of winds and currents that several mil-lennia earlier brought Jōmon fishermen to the Ecuadorian shore, the cultural context was very different. In China and India, urban civilization was well established by the beginning of the Christian Era. Trading vessels capable of carrying 600 men and 1000 metric tons of cargo made long voyages out of sight of land, exchanging produce between the mainland and colonies in South East Asia and Indonesia. If disabled, such a ship would have been amply provisioned to sustain its pas-sengers during a long period of drift.

From the Ecuadorian point of view, these immigrants would have arrived at an opportune time. By the early part of the Bahía Phase, agricultural techniques were well enough de-veloped to ensure a relatively stable and abundant food supply. Increased productivity would have permitted a certain pro-portion of the population to engage full time in non-subsistence activities, as artisans, priests or administrators. With the passage of time, developing ceremonial practices would have become crystallized and resistant to change. As it was, they were still pliant. We can guess little more than the fact that a transpacific contact took place, but the secretive smile on one La Plata Seated figurine suggests that he could tell a fascinating story, if only he could speak.

Emilio Estrada, who was an amateur sailor as well as archaeologist, noted that to reach La Plata from the southern Manabí coast required tacking because of the contrary winds. From this he inferred that the ancient Bahians were skilful sailors. Evidence that they may have been beneficiaries of a

Plate 26

transpacific contact is the more interesting because of similarities between rafts navigated by sails and movable centre-boards on the Ecuadorian coast and those on the coasts of South East Asia. Although the destructive climate may never permit direct confirmation, the hypothesis that sailing rafts were among the cultural traits introduced at this time helps to account not only for the apparently greater seaward mobility of the Bahians, but for the florescence of maritime activity under their successors, the Manteño.

The pottery, like that of other Regional Developmental Phases, combines features traceable to a Formative heritage with new elements either locally developed or reflecting influence from the outside. The principal Chorrera Phase survivals are iridescent painting and flaring-rim bowls, while other common decorative techniques such as nicked-shoulder embellishment and zoned hachure resemble Machalilla Phase types. Burnished-line designs in broad parallel bands or finer cross-hatch patterns, red-on-buff painting, and negative painting are techniques shared with other contemporary phases. Distinctive Bahía Phase specializations are nicked-and-perforated rim embellishments, incision filled after firing with red, yellow or white pigment, and polychrome (red and black) painting on a plain or white-slipped surface. Incision on an unpolished surface defines zones painted after firing in red, yellow, green, white and black. Although polished red-slipped vessels are frequent, white-on-red painting appears to be absent.

The commonest vessel shapes are shallow bowls with broad out-sloping or horizontal rims, and conical, cylindrical or bifurcated polypod legs, sometimes anthropomorphized. Low annular bases also occur, but tall pedestal compoteras are rare. Bottles with a free-standing spout, or a spout attached to a handle in the Chorrera Phase tradition, are relatively common. Jars have globular bodies or angular shoulders, constricted mouths and everted rims. Cylindrical jars have a flat bottom and an anthropomorphic figure ornamenting one side. Grater bowls have interiors roughened by punctation.

While objects of Bahía Phase origin have been encountered in sites of all the other Regional Developmental Period cultures, reciprocal evidence of contact is limited. Figurines of Guangala and Jama⁄Coaque Phase origin are most common in sites closest to the frontiers shared with these phases. The presence of Guangala Phase anthropomorphic polypod legs and Jama⁄Coaque mammiform legs indicates that bowls were sometimes also acquired. Post⁄fired painting may be an introduction from the Jama⁄Coaque Phase, where it is more highly developed.

THE JAMA⁄COAQUE PHASE

Between Cape San Francisco and the Bahía de Caráquez, the terrain is rolling, densely forested and drained by small streams usually navigable only for short distances inland. There are no large modern towns, and a few dry⁄weather roads provide access only to the southern half of the region. Little archaeological work has been done, but existing evidence suggests that this was one of the most highly developed portions of the coast during the Regional Developmental Period.

All known sites are accumulations of habitation refuse, containing abundant sherds of vessels and figurines, pottery artifacts, and fragments of shell and stone, including chips of obsidian. Refuse covers an area about 100 by 20 metres at several sites, while in others it is concentrated on a steep slope, suggesting a dump used by a village on the summit. Depth of accumulation may reach 1·50 metres. Shells, including mangrove oyster, indicate that this subsistence resource continued to supplement a diet based principally on cultivated plants. Direct evidence of village layout and house construction is lacking, but one house model shows a front opening and a slightly

Fig. 32a

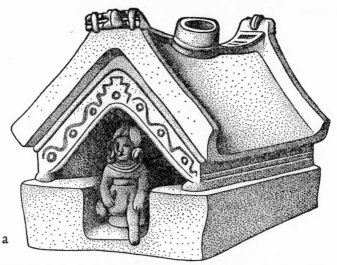

a

Fig. 32. Similarities between house type of Ecuador and Palau. a. House-shaped vessel from Jama with negative painting on the gable; b. Palau house with similar gable decoration

b

97

curved ridge crossed by short poles like models from the Bahía Phase. Painted ornamentation along the gable is done in the negative technique, while the rear has an all-over design in green, yellow and red post-fired painting. Like Bahía Phase house models, details repeat those on houses across the Pacific, in this instance, on the island of Palau.

Stone tools are no better made than in other Regional Developmental phases, and carved stone blocks and tusk amulets like those of the Bahía Phase do not occur. Although figurines wear elaborate ornaments, the ornaments themselves are rarely encountered in the refuse. A few metal objects, including some elaborate gold head-dresses, have come from northern Manabí, but whether they are assignable to this or the following period has not been established.

Pottery artifacts are abundant and well made. Spindle whorls, head-rests, flat and cylindrical stamps, bird and animal whistles, and tubular flutes are particularly numerous. Stamps display a variety of complicated patterns interweaving geometrical and zoomorphic motifs, many with Mesoamerican parallels. Rarer artifacts include low stools with a slightly concave circular top and four plump cylindrical legs, and elbow tobacco pipes. The bowl is usually located in the body of a human or animal figure, but some pipes take the form of a human arm with the mouthpiece in the extended thumb. Also characteristic are small masks with realistic or stylized human faces. Although the eyes or eye-balls are usually perforated, use is problematical since they are far too small to be worn by people and too large to fit most figurines. Perforations at the upper edge suggest they may have been attached to a garment. Height is usually between 8 and 15 cm.

Figurines are typically mould-made, either completely or as a preliminary to the addition of appliqué. Estrada has suggested a classification based on eye treatment. The Chone type, which is most common, is identified by an eye in the shape of a

Fig. 32b

Plate 39

Plates 35, 36

Plate 34

Plate 31

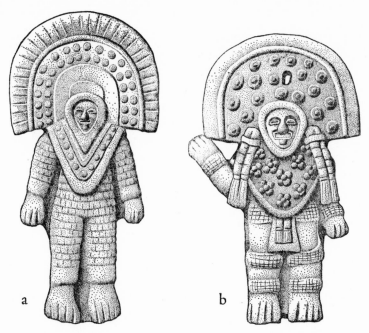

Fig. 33 Male figurines of the Chone type with elaborate costume and head-dress. a. Feather suit; b. Short bib-like poncho and loin-cloth. The D-shaped eye and labret at the lower lip are diagnostic of the Chone type

D with the flat edge down, produced by a combination of relief and incision. The mouth is usually of similar construc-tion but rectanguloid in outline, with a circular labret adjacent to the lower edge. Both male and female versions occur, each with a wide variety of head-dresses, ornaments and body cover-ings. Also represented are winged monsters, with head and body following the style of female figurines, and animals with elaborate and intricate costumes and head-dresses.

Male figurines include two striking varieties. One wears trousers and a long-sleeved shirt apparently made of feather-covered fabric, and a large head-dress completely surrounding the face, which peers through an opening. Hands and feet are bare. A second frequently portrayed costume is a loin-cloth

Plate 27

Plate 28

Fig. 33a

Fig. 33b

with a wide flap at the front and a short sleeveless poncho, sometimes extending only to the waist like a bib. This poncho is elaborately fringed, appliquéd and painted, suggesting richly ornamented fabric. Head-dress is variable, sometimes framing the face, at other times fitting closely to the head like a bonnet. Tassels often hang down from the ears as far as the waist. Wide, thick bands encircle the leg below the knee and at the ankle. Although typically standing, some examples are seated.

Plate 25   Female figurines are much less ornately dressed and ornamented. Some are nude, while others wear a short straight skirt. Posture is standing or kneeling. The usual necklace is a thick, wide collar, apparently composed of many strands of minute beads. Smaller multiple strings are worn as bracelets. The top

Fig. 34   of the head is slightly to markedly swept back and the head-dress is smooth or simply ornamented, most frequently with a long 'flap' extending downward over the shoulders at each side behind the ears, which contain a row of solid or perforated studs, or are fringed with small rings.

Plate 22   Other Jama-Coaque Phase eye treatments include a D-shaped outline set at a slant instead of horizontally and a relief oval. Complete arms with a rounded shoulder perforated for attachment to a body attest the existence of figurines with movable limbs.

Plate 32, left   Several figurines combine human and animal traits. One head has a modified D-shaped eye and a gaping rectanguloid mouth dominated by long tusk-like canine teeth projecting upward from the lower jaw and downward from the upper one.

Plate 33   A sphinx-like creature has a nearly human head except for the up-curved nose, a mouth filled with fearsome teeth, and an animal body with a serrated dorsal ridge and a stubby tail.

It is evident that these figurines depict the dress and ornament of daily life as well as costumes appropriate to ceremonial occasions. Both modelling and painting suggest a well-developed art in textiles and featherwork. Although metal counterparts

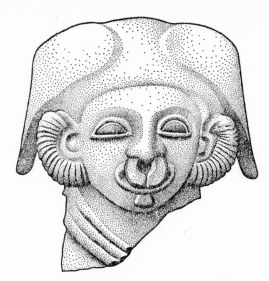

Fig. 34. Female figurine head of the Chone type with a large nose-ring and rings fringing the rim of each ear

have not been found, nose, lip and ear ornaments as well as occasional elaborate pendants or pectorals take forms typically executed in gold or copper in Colombia, suggesting that metallurgy too may have been practised. Extensive use of moulds for figurine manufacture implies a demand requiring mass production for its satisfaction, perhaps carried out by specialists. Numerous beautifully designed flat and cylindrical stamps may have been used for body painting or for ornamentation of textiles. The well-made pipes suggest ritual use of tobacco.

The pottery has not been systematically analysed, so that only a few characteristics can be described. Among decorative techniques are fine incision either in single or paired lines forming graceful curvilinear patterns on a red-slipped surface, negative painting, and post-fired painting in red, yellow, green, white and black. Cylindrical jars may have a figurine of the Chone type moulded on one side. Other vessel shapes include rounded and angular-shouldered jars, often with a short spout, and flat-bottomed, vertical-walled bowls. Small shallow bowls with bulbous mammiform tripod legs occur, as well as conical,

Plate 24

101

cylindrical and loop legs. A form not represented to the south is a jar with two out-sloping spouts connected by a bridge handle.

Trade items reflecting contact with contemporary Ecuadorian cultures are difficult to identify at the present state of knowledge. The fact that the Jama-Coaque Phase shares a number of traits with the Bahía Phase to the south and the Tolita Phase in Esmeraldas indicates the existence of a generalized intercommunication zone along the northern coast. Some kinds of objects, such as head-rests, and certain types of figurines may be assignable to trade origin when the whole area is better known.

Numerous elements of the Jama-Coaque complex have parallels in Mesoamerica. The elaborate feather costumes, and many other details of dress and ornament are strikingly similar. Liberal application of green, yellow, black and white paint is a typical Mesoamerican practice. Small pottery masks and flat and cylinder stamps are present in Mesoamerica from the Early Formative Period. The closeness of the resemblance and the greater antiquity of most of the traits in Mexico indicate that contact between the Ecuadorian coast and Mesoamerica was re-established in the early part of the Regional Developmental Period. Communication was apparently maintained thereafter, leading to the exchange of important cultural elements over subsequent centuries. Whether contacts took the form of relatively regular trading expeditions or infrequent and sporadic voyages may become clear after more archaeological work has been done, both in Ecuador and on the Pacific coast of Mesoamerica.

THE TOLITA PHASE

The far northern coast is archaeologically the most famous part of Ecuador. Figurines, stamps and other objects have found their way into museums and houses around the world, and the best illustrated publications on Ecuadorian archaeology, by Uhle, d'Harcourt, Verneau and Rivet, deal principally with Esmeraldas Province. In spite of this renown, the Esmeraldas coast is one of the most poorly known areas with respect to chronology. No stratigraphical excavations have been pub-lished, and few specimens have specific identification of source. The most famous site, La Tolita, has been mercilessly looted on a commercial basis for its goldwork in one of the most tragic episodes in New World archaeology.

La Tolita occupies the southern part of one of the larger islands in the mouth of the Río Santiago, not far from the Colombian border. When it was visited by Saville at the be-ginning of the century, it was in the process of being cleared for pasture, exposing some forty artificial mounds of varying size and height. The rectanguloid surface of the highest reached 9 metres over a 20 by 45 metre area. One larger mound, with an area 25 by 82 metres, was only 2 metres high. The remainder were circular, ovoid or irregular in outline and between 1·5 and 7·5 metres high. Several, including the highest, appeared to be arranged around a 190 metre-wide plaza, while others were scattered along the river bank.

What is unusual and puzzling about La Tolita is the abun-dance of vessel and figurine fragments throughout the area, around and between the mounds to a depth of a metre and a half, as well as in the earth of which they are constructed. This has led several investigators to suggest that the figurines and other refuse belong to an early occupation, and were gathered up by later residents along with the earth during construction of the mounds. Such an interpretation tallies with evidence in the Guayas basin that mound-building is late, whereas figurines are abundant in the Regional Developmental Period.

If the mounds are relegated to later occupation, the site of La Tolita does not differ greatly except in size from sites of the Jama-Coaque Phase, where figurines and other artifacts abound in the village refuse. Smaller sites of similar nature are reported along the coast and the banks of the Río Verde, Río Mates and Río Ostiones. Subsistence patterns were probably similar to those of contemporary groups to the south. As today, the rivers and sea were undoubtedly the main routes of communication as well as an important source of food. Hunting probably sup-plemented manioc, maize and other cultivated crops. Graters of pottery and trough-shaped stone *metates* reflect methods of food preparation.

Two pottery vessels from the Río Mates depict architectural features. One has a saddle roof and cross-pieces along the ridge resembling models from the Bahía and Jama-Coaque Phases, but the usual solid wall is replaced by a row of columns resting on circular bases. The second model shows a square house with intersecting straight ridge poles and four gables, each rising from the ground level at the sides. A model from La Tolita has a flight of steps leading to the front door, while the sides and back drop vertically, corresponding to Jijón y Caamaño's description of Bahía Phase platforms at Manta. An ovoid floor plan is shown on a jar, but this is perhaps attributable to the vessel body contour.

Hundreds of small metal objects have been salvaged from La Tolita, mixed with sherds, figurine fragments and other cul-tural refuse. Analysis of their composition and method of manu-facture by Paul Bergsøe showed the copper and gold to be of high purity, leading him to conclude that virgin metal was used. Alluvial gold mixed with platinum and silver occurs in the vicinity, but a source of pure copper ore is as yet unknown. Rings, nose-rings, a variety of pins and studs with ornamental heads, needles, bells, miniature masks, dangles, beads, and fish-hooks of gold or copper are characteristic. The only large objects are copper axes of rectanguloid outline with a curved, slightly expanded blade. Silver was unknown, but lead and platinum were occasionally used.

Plate 38

Plate 37

Careful analysis of the composition and technology by Bergsøe shows that the remarkable nature of some of the objects is more a reflection of skill and manual dexterity on the part of the makers than of advanced metallurgical techniques. Artisans were unable to melt more than 30 gr. with a blowpipe and charcoal, but this method was sufficient to extract small amounts of lead from galena, to alloy gold with copper to be used for fusion gilding of copper objects, to weld, and to draw enough gold into platinum to create a workable alloy. The other principal technique was hammering, which flattened small nuggets into sheets, and when applied to heated metal hardened as well as shaped it. Having reproduced all of the kinds of objects recovered from La Tolita, both in composition and form, Bergsøe concluded that specialized artisans were not required. The wide variation in calibre of workmanship and the lack of standardization also indicated to him that each man had his own metalworking kit.

Pottery artifacts resemble those of the JamaCoaque Phase. Small masks usually depict human faces similar in style to those of the figurines. The eyes are not always perforated. Cylindrical and flat stamps, the latter circular, square or asymmetrical in outline are indistinguishable from those of the JamaCoaque Phase. Musical instruments include bird, animal and anthropomorphic whistles, both hand and mouldmade, as well as flutes and Panpipes. Spindle whorls, usually of the turret form, and plain or decorated with incision, imply spinning, probably of cotton. Fishshaped graters, roughened either by deep punctation or by embedding small stones, must have performed some ceremonial function since they seem too small to have been practical for daily food preparation. A number of miniature vessels, beautifully excised, incised or modelled in anthropomorphic and zoomorphic forms, hint at special practices; but whether these were ceremonial or cosmetic we have no means of telling.

Plate 31

Most varied and abundant are figurines. In spite of mass production in moulds, the majority exhibit a naturalism in expression and anatomy that contrasts with the stiffness and stylization characteristic of other coastal cultures. Nose-rings are common but not universal. Ear ornamentation is character-istic and varied, including a perforated bead or a napkin-ring in the lobe, a series of rings, perforated beads or perforations along the outer edge of the ear, a short tassel or linked ring hanging from the lobe, and perforated beads filling the ear cavity. Ornamentation of the lower lip is rare, but a stud at each side of the nose is often shown, suggesting the use made of small gold studs that abound in the refuse at La Tolita.

Plate 29

Female figurines wear a short straight skirt, plain or orna-mented with incision, leaving the upper body bare. On male figurines a loin-cloth is substituted for the skirt. A bib-like poncho or a simple turban head-dress may also be worn. A more elaborate costume, probably of ceremonial significance, takes the form of a skirt of wide strips covering a loin-cloth, while the face peers out through the gaping mouth of an animal head-dress with a large lolling tongue. Hand-modelled figurines also occur, many of high artistic merit. Some heads approach life-size.

In addition to figurines there are two kinds of mould-made plaques. One takes the form of a nude male lying on his back, with broad strips of cloth binding his arms to his sides. The other shows a man and woman, sometimes accompanied by a child, or an adult and a child, often embracing. Some have perforations suggesting they may have been worn as pendants.

Semi-zoomorphic depictions are common, usually animal- or bird-headed and human-bodied. Perhaps these represent humans masquerading as gods. Many figurines stand with one

Plate 32

arm outstretched. Fanged monsters repeat a Jama-Coaque Phase theme. The so-called 'alter ego' motif can be recognized in the superposition of a second head on top of the normal one.

The pottery has not been carefully studied, but what is known indicates that it departs considerably from that characteristic of the southern Regional Developmental complexes. White-on-red painting has not been reported, but white and red occurs either separately or combined with negative painting. Red-on-buff, angular red zones defined by incised lines, and fine incision on a red-slipped surface are typical. A common embellishment is a flange around the vessel waist or a little below the rim. Diagnostic shapes include two out-sloping spouts joined by a curved bridge handle, jars and bowls with hollow bulbous tripod legs, annular-based jars with a generally cylindrical form obscured by bulges and flanges, and shallow bowls made in a mould producing decorations resembling incision. Rounded and carinated bowls, polypod bowls and compoteras are among utilitarian forms.

Trade objects that might provide clues to chronological correlations are difficult to recognize because of the generally poor data regarding source and absence of detailed description of the local products. However, a few figurines with the diagnostic Chone D-shaped eye are reported from La Tolita, and miniature anthropomorphic vessels from the Río Ostiones are identical to specimens from Jama-Coaque Phase sites. Also linking the two Phases are the flat and cylindrical stamps, one of the latter from La Tolita bearing the circle-and-dot pattern characteristic of stone plaques from the Bahía Phase. Such cross-ties will probably become increasingly evident with additional work.

THE TIAONE PHASE

The region between Cape San Francisco and the mouth of the Río Esmeraldas, is the most poorly known portion of the coast. Figurines appear to be less common than to the north and south and pottery characteristics are different. Several sites along the Río Tiaone have produced shallow, thin-walled bowls with a polished red slip and hollow bulbous polypod legs, often modelled to suggest stylized birds. Parallel narrow red stripes on a buff surface are the most commonly reported kind of decoration. Graters have incised, cross/hatched roughening. Figurines include a hand/modelled type, seated with legs out/ stretched. One body represents the La Plata Seated type with the legs laid one above the other, establishing contemporaneity between the Bahía and Tiaone Phases, as well as the existence of trade relations between them.

THE CHAULLABAMBA PHASE

Although a large number of archaeological sites have been reported from the Cuenca basin, few have been described in detail or systematically investigated. Stratigraphic excavations by Collier and Murra at Cerro Narrío in the Cañar valley and by Bennett at Monjashuaico in the Paute area, as well as sur/ veys by these and other investigators, indicate the presence of a ceramic complex typologically equivalent to those associated with coastal phases of the Regional Developmental Period. The names of the best/known sites, Cerro Narrío, Monjashuaico and Huancarcuchu, have been applied to such specific cultural assemblages as to make them unsuitable for designation of the generalized phase. Hence, Chaullabamba, a name earlier pro/ posed by Uhle, has been adopted here.

Habitation sites of the Chaullabamba Phase are not only numerous in the Cuenca basin, but have been reported to the north in the Cañar valley and to the south on the head/ waters of the Río Jubones. Both the Jubones and the Río Naranjal flow to the southern coast, providing routes of com/ munication along which influences passed, to judge from similarities between highland and lowland ceramic complexes. A spill/over to the eastern slopes is indicated by a site on the Río Upano, from which a carbon/14 date of 620 ± 440 BC has been obtained. Sites are typically along river banks between 2000 and 3000 metres in elevation, although a few occupy rock-shelters. The area appears to be small, but no measurements are specified. Refuse accumulation reaches about 1·5 metres. No burials are reported.

Cerro Narrío is a barren steep-sided hill, the end of a spur overlooking the Cañar valley. Occupation refuse covers the whole hill, an area some 175 by 375 metres, but early remains are confined to the slopes. Charred remnants provide direct evidence of maize cultivation, probably on the fertile valley floor, while numerous deer and rabbit bones indicate that hunting continued to be an important activity. Post-holes suggest that houses were oval or circular.

Artifacts are not abundant in Chaullabamba Phase sites, a situation reminiscent of that in the Guayas basin. Stone implements are particularly rare. Bone awls are common, and together with sherd spindle whorls imply the manufacture of cord and textiles. Ornaments are of particular interest because they are principally made from marine shells, including spondylus and clam, which could only have been acquired from the coast. They were shaped into beads, pendants and crude figurines, some of which have 'alter ego' treatment. Stone beads also occur.

Pottery figurines are rare and fragmentary. Flat and cylindrical stamps of pottery are reported from some sites, but are rare. Pottery stools, 10 cm. high and 25 cm. in diameter at the concave circular top, seem to be associated with this phase. They are painted red on buff, white on red, or white and red, sometimes accompanied by incision. The top always has a perforation in the centre. Although Cerro Narrío is notorious for its treasure, Collier and Murra found no metal objects in levels equating with the early occupation, so that the existence of metal-working is not confirmed although it can be assumed to have been present.

Pottery is well-made, with fine paste, thin walls, and even, often polished surfaces. Buff is the typical colour and red on buff the most common style of decoration. Polished red slip is also frequent. Red-on-buff designs include wide and narrow bands and larger solid zones. Polishing was subsequent to painting, and bands not paralleling the horizontal polishing strokes frequently show the blurred edges characteristic of earlier Machalilla Phase red bands. Zones between bands may be filled with painted or punctate dots, and bands may be de-limited by incised lines. White-on-red designs executed in bands and dots occur alone or combined with negative painting. Other decorative techniques include negative on a red or plain polished surface, red finger-painting, burnished lines on an un-polished surface, and fine incision on a polished or unpolished surface. A few iridescent-painted sherds have been reported from Cerro Narrío. Zoomorphic relief heads and nicked appliqué ribs are rare.

The commonest vessel shapes are globular, everted-rim jars and rounded bowls, the latter sometimes with a low annular base. Mildly carinated and flat-based, cylindrical bowls also occur. Tripod, polypod, tall pedestal-based forms and bottles are not reported. An unusual jar has a short concave or vertical neck, its mouth closed except for a small round hole.

In addition to the decorative techniques that equate the Chaullabamba Phase to coastal ceramic complexes of the Regional Developmental Period, there is evidence of trade re-lations between the two areas. Objects of marine shell are the best examples, since the raw material could only have been acquired from the coast. Several sherds from Cerro Narrío be-long to carinated bowls with zoned-punctate decoration on the upper wall, which duplicate in both form and decoration typical vessels of the Daule Phase. The rarity of iridescent-painted sherds suggests they may also have been acquired by trade from the coast.

THE TUNCAHUÁN PHASE

The name 'Tuncahuán', taken from a cemetery site in the province of Chimborazo, has been used by Jijón y Caamaño and others to designate the combination of negative and red painting regardless of where it appears. Since this technique probably did not originate in the Tuncahuán region, and since it persisted until the Conquest in several parts of Ecuador, it seems preferable to reserve the term for the Regional Develop' mental cultural complex in the Tuncahuán area.

Sites of the Tuncahuán Phase have been reported so far only from the Riobamba basin, along the Río Chambo and up the slopes below 3000 metres. To the east and west, the mountains rise above 4000 metres, incorporating several snow'capped peaks. A pass connects the head'waters of the Chambo with tributaries of the Milagro and Yaguachi rivers flowing west' ward into the lower Río Guayas. To the east, the Chambo enters the Río Pastaza, which decends into the Amazonian lowlands.

The type site is a cemetery of pit graves, five of which were excavated by Jijón. The pits were 1·20 to 2·50 metres deep, and those with identifiable remains contained a single skeleton. Except for a child, with which no artifacts were buried, grave goods included pottery vessels and copper objects. A large disk'headed pin and a loop with the ends curving toward each side into spirals were hammered from copper, and the conical sheath for the end of a spear'thrower and its animal'head hook may have been manufactured in the same way. The only other grave object is a hollow anthropomorphic pottery figure with a globular body and a rounded head (arms and legs are broken off).

Pottery decoration is by three principal techniques. White dots, crosses and spirals on a red'slipped surface duplicate patterns of coastal Regional Developmental Period complexes.

III

Also typical of the coast are concentric bands, alternating red and white, on bowl interiors. Negative painting in dots and bands on a plain or red-slipped surface repeats motifs of coastal iridescent-painted designs. Negative patterns may be embellished by white lines and rings, another coastal technique. A further three-colour combination is produced by addition of red bands to accent a negative-decorated vessel – the technique that has become synonymous with Tuncahuán. Red painting on a plain surface also occurs.

Typical vessel shapes include rounded or slightly angular bowls and jars, sometimes with a small flattened base. Also characteristic are tall compoteras, some with a rattle base, and bowls with a low annular base. Both types of base may have cut-out sections for ornamental effect. Tripod or polypod supports are not reported.

THE NORTHERN HIGHLANDS

No complexes combining the horizon markers of white-on-red and negative painting are identifiable in publications on the highlands north of the Riobamba basin. It is improbable that the Quito and Ibarra basins were uninhabited by settled agriculturalists, and several explanations can be suggested for this lack of evidence. The spectacular nature of Integration Period remains may have caused simpler sites to be overlooked. On the other hand, the pottery may continue the postulated Early Formative highland tradition without incorporating the horizon decorative techniques so that complexes have not been recognized as belonging to the Regional Developmental Period. A third possibility is that the principal source of influences was the Esmeraldas coast, where the horizon markers are rare. These and other alternative explanations cannot be evaluated until systematic work has been done and a reliable chronological sequence established in the northern basins.

LOCAL VARIATION DURING THE REGIONAL
DEVELOPMENTAL PERIOD

The archaeological phases of the Regional Developmental Period align themselves into two general groups. The southern one includes the Guangala, Tejar, Daule, Jambelí, Chaullabamba and Tuncahuán Phases, occupying the area in which earlier Chorrera Phase remains have been found with the addition of the Riobamba basin and the exception of the central Manabí coast. Within this geographical range, varying combinations of elevation, soil, temperature and rainfall interacted with processes of cultural evolution to create distinctive local cultures. The existence of natural buffer zones in the form of *Fig. 19* swampy, arid or mountainous terrain promoted relative isolation, enhancing the possibility for differentiation from the ancestral Chorrera Phase. These buffer zones probably served as hunting territories and as the source of various other kinds of natural resources. That regional isolation was not complete is clearly demonstrated by the existence of traded objects in most of the phases.

The settlement pattern continues that of the Chorrera Phase, with small clusters of thatch-roofed houses scattered along the river banks. As population increased, it was dispersed by the creation of new hamlets, so that settlement was always near to both fields and streams, which provided both a supplementary source of food and a water supply. This scattered pattern would not have been safe had raiding or warfare been practised and, added to the lack of evidence of preference for easily defended locations (except for Cerro Narrío on a high hilltop), suggests that these regional phases were typically at peace with one another.

Also missing from the southern phases is evidence of marked social stratification. Although distinctions undoubtedly existed in status and rank, the coercive power of higher-ranking individuals was probably minimal. Evidence of religion is slight, and here the contrast with the elaboration in figurines and other ritual objects on the north coast is most marked. While it can, not be assumed that the supernatural played no important role in the lives of the more southerly groups, it was probably a less dominating force.

Except in the highlands, the warm tropical climate made clothing unnecessary, and on most occasions none was prob, ably worn. Cotton was known, but spindle whorls of pottery are rare and there is evidence that bark cloth was manufactured in addition to woven cloth. In the highlands, the presence in a Tuncahuán Phase grave of a flat,headed pin (*tupu*), used in later times to fasten a shawl, suggests that this article of dress was already in existence, probably worn in addition to a loin, cloth or skirt. Personal attractiveness was enhanced by neck, laces of shell and stone beads, nose,rings, and a variety of ear ornaments, sometimes made from beaten gold or copper as well as perishable materials.

While utility jars are typically large and thick,walled, smaller containers are thin,walled, with graceful forms and polished surfaces. Tall compoteras and rounded or flaring goblets with low pedestals sometimes containing rattles are characteristic shapes. In addition to the horizon decorative techniques, white,on,red and negative painting, various kinds of incised and red,banded decoration were widely employed.

The Guangala Phase, occupying the portion of the coast ex, posed to transpacific and Mesoamerican influences during the Formative Period, has characteristics suggesting that outsiders continued to be cast upon Ecuadorian shores. Certain Guan, gala Phase traits, such as mould,made figurines and pottery stamps, can be ascribed to contact with the neighbouring Bahía Phase. However, the brilliant polychrome painting and the burnished,line decoration are unique in Ecuador and have their closest parallels in Costa Rica and the Nazca valley of southern Peru. Careful analysis of the total cultural context and chronologies of these widely separated regions should permit reconstruction of the manner in which the similarities came about.

The northern group of regional complexes, including the Bahía, Jama-Coaque, Tiaone and Tolita Phases, differs markedly from that to the south. Part of the contrast stems from the slightness of the Chorrera Phase influence on the pottery, which provides a unifying heritage for members of the southern group, and part from the failure of the horizon techniques of pottery decoration to achieve major popularity. The dominant factor, however, is strong Mesoamerican influence, which introduced alien practices that contrast sharply with the general pattern of culture in the Andean Area.

The settlement pattern was least affected. Small clusters of houses along the shore and river banks are characteristic, but larger centres occur in which some buildings were constructed on low dirt platforms with a ramp or staircase at one end. House models suggest that such buildings had deep saddle roofs with ornamental projections and painted walls. Structures of a defensive nature have not been reported.

Strongest evidence of social stratification comes from differences in dress and ornament of the figurines. Daily dress for men was a loin-cloth and for women a short straight skirt. Both sexes wore necklaces, bracelets, anklets, nose- and earrings. In the Jama-Coaque region lip ornaments were common, while the Tolita people favoured round gold studs embedded at each side of the nose. Flat and roller stamps may have been used for applying patterns to textiles or the skin. Some individuals wear this basic costume but add a head-dress with long flaps at the sides, horn-like projections from the top, or asymmetrical relief and painted decoration. Elaborate costumes, probably worn by chiefs or priests, include a feather-covered suit, an ornately decorated poncho, and enormous head-dresses apparently constructed of textiles and feathers on a basketry foundation.

There is little doubt that religion was a potent force on the northern coast during this period, not only in providing a basis for social stratification and control, but in more personal ways. Many small figurines are perforated to be worn as amulets, and plaques with family groups may have had magical significance. The mass of hand- and mould-made figurines have no obvious explanation. Many may have served as household deities, since they occur abundantly in village refuse. On the other hand their concentration on La Plata Island, where no one apparently lived, cannot be accounted for in this way. Numerous half-animal figures may symbolize a god's special powers. Jaguars, birds, snakes, and fanged demons are commonly represented. Pipes, amulets, stools, head-rests, house models, stone carvings and masks are other possible ritual objects.

Pottery vessel forms are characterized by tripod and polypod bowls, with legs ranging from bulbous-mammiform to slender tapering outline. Bowls and bottles may have flat bases. Jars are often narrow-mouthed. Single- or double-spouted bottles may have double or tripartite bodies. Low annular bases occur, but compoteras are rare. Except in the Bahía Phase, decoration is mostly by incision either alone or in conjunction with post-fired polychrome or pre-fired red painting. A few mould-made bowls are reported from the Tolita Phase, otherwise manufacture was by coiling.

Mesoamerican influence is strongest on the Tolita Phase. Diagnostic artifacts with prototypes in Vera Cruz, Oaxaca, and the valley of Mexico include pottery masks, cylindrical and flat stamps, mould-made figurines with feather costumes, animal head-dresses with gaping mouth, plaques depicting couples, family groups or bound figures, demons and semi-anthropo-morphic creatures, post-fired painting in green, black, white and yellow, and numerous other specific details. Whether this acculturation was produced by a colony of Mesoamericans in Esmeraldas, or reflects a trading relationship of a continuing nature, or resulted from some other kind of contact is a question that must await future work in both areas for an answer. Whatever the explanation, northern Esmeraldas seems to be the focus of concentration for Mesoamerican traits, which become less frequent and more modified in form with increasing distance to the north and south.

Within the Tolita Phase area, the site of La Tolita stands out. The abundance of figurines and metal objects in the refuse suggests a specialized function, while the frequency of potsherds and utensils of daily life indicates that it was also a place of habitation for a considerable number of people. The quantity of gold ornaments makes it apparent that they were worn by everyone, not reserved to a few members of the community. Their frequency is so much greater than at other Tolita Phase sites, however, as to suggest that all residents may have had special status, perhaps as functionaries of a ceremonial centre. Also favouring this interpretation is the location of La Tolita in swampy terrain, following the pattern of ceremonial centres of the Mexican Vera Cruz coast, with which many of the figurines and other traits of material culture are allied.

The Bahía Phase, at the southern edge of the zone of Mesoamerican influence, shows signs of contact with an even more distant region. La Plata Seated figurines have Asian prototypes, as do small house models with exotic architecture, tusk-shaped amulets, pottery head-rests, Pan-pipes graduated from both sides toward the centre, and 'golf-tee' ear plugs of pottery. The sailing raft navigated by movable centre-boards, also common in South East Asia, may have been the craft that brought a second group of accidental Asian immigrants to the Ecuadorian shore. That the Bahía Phase people may have been pre-eminent seafarers during this period is suggested by their use of La Plata Island as a ceremonial sanctuary, and also by the presence of artifacts of Bahía Phase origin in all of the other contemporary coastal complexes. Such a combination of commercial and religious interests would account for the greater urbanism achieved along the central Manabí coast, and might have created a sociopolitical organization more secular in content than the theocratic emphasis apparently developed to the north.

Around AD 500, the regional cultures began to be integrated into larger configurations. The manner in which this came about, and the factors contributing to the change are obscure. Territorial expansion is characteristic of agricultural societies at a certain stage of development; why it happened when it did on the Ecuadorian coast may be understood when the paleoclimatology is better known. There is a suggestion that parts of the area suffered reduction in rainfall, which could have led to local crop failure and pressure for new land. Whatever the dynamic factors may have been, the result was the emergence of a totally different configuration by around AD 700.

CHAPTER VI

The Integration Period

GENERAL CHARACTERISTICS

URING THE FINAL MILLENNIUM of aboriginal cultural development, trends discernible during the preceding
period became more marked. Increasingly reliable agricultural
techniques permitted population expansion, and habitation
sites are more numerous than at any other time. Several are large
enough to be classified as urban centres. Occupational division
of labour became more extensive and differences in rank more
pronounced. Attention was turned from adaptation to the
existing environment toward its improvement, with the result
that slopes were terraced, wells dug and artificial mounds constructed. Pottery declines in artistic quality, partly as a result of
mass production and partly because of the shift to other materials, especially metal, for the manufacture of prestige objects.
Figurines, whistles, stamps and other pottery artifacts become
rare. Spindle whorls, by contrast, are extremely abundant,
implying greatly increased production of textiles of cotton and
wool. Copper supplements stone for the manufacture of axes,
adzes, knives and club heads, in addition to its use along with
silver and gold for ornaments and smaller utensils. For the first
time a few surviving fragments provide direct evidence of accomplishments in textiles, basketry and wood carving. These
and other goods are preserved in cemeteries, which provide
much indirect information on sociopolitical and religious
patterns as well as quantities of complete pottery vessels. The
first Spaniards to set foot on Ecuadorian soil in the early decades of the sixteenth century provide eye-witness accounts that
supplement archaeological inferences.

Pottery is characterized by distinctive decorative techniques
and vessel forms. Domestic jars are plain, thick-walled and

Fig. 35

much larger than in the preceding period. Bowls and jars often have flat bases. Annular-based jars are typical, but globular jars with tall tripod legs are most diagnostic. Compoteras remain popular, and a tall slender form is a late time-marker. Symmetry is often poor and surface finish uneven. Decoration is relatively simple and standardized, with incision, combing, line burnishing, red banding and appliqué the most common techniques. Negative painting, often with the addition of red bands, reaches its maximum elaboration. Anthropomorphic jars, which are nearly universal, typically show the addition of facial features to the vessel's neck without modification of the body toward human form and rarely with the addition of limbs. Faces are usually stylized, although exceptions attest the skill of the potters at realistic portrayal.

Metallurgy shows technological advance in the handling of copper and silver, which require different methods from those used in working gold. Copper was sufficiently abundant to be cast into large objects and to be used for needles, tweezers, fish-hooks and a variety of other everyday tools. Copper earrings and nose-rings were the ornaments of the commoner, while individuals of higher status wore silver and gold.

The most striking change in the non-technological realm of culture is the practice of burial in shaft-and-chamber tombs or pottery urns, often grouped in cemeteries. The deceased was provided with objects for his comfort in the next world in keeping with his status and occupation during life. Important chiefs were provided not only with quantities of rich material goods, but often with wives and retainers as well.

Growing sociopolitical complexity and occupational specialization brought a need for accurate measurement and standards of value. Like their neighbours to the south, the aboriginal Ecuadorians did not develop writing, nor did they adopt the *quipu* or knotted cord used by the Inca for keeping records. For commercial transactions where measurement of quantity was

Fig. 35. Diagnostic vessel shapes of the Integration Period

important, as in weighing gold, a steelyard was employed. A thin axe-shaped copper sheet with a rib around the edge served as a medium of exchange, and copper or silver rings and heavy copper plaques may represent other standards of value.

Warfare, the handmaiden of civilization, can be detected archaeologically for the first time in the appearance of stone and copper club heads, useful only against a human quarry. Lances, slings, wooden swords and spear-throwers were also used. Large armies could be mustered when needed for defence, and their strength and skill were sufficient to hold back the Inca for several years in the north highlands. On the coast, Spanish sources recount the strategy of the wily Puná Indians in their continuing hostilities with the residents of Tumbes on the north Peruvian coast.

The extent to which the archaeological phases of the Integration Period represent integrated sociopolitical units is impossible to determine at present. Spanish listings of tribes and linguistic groups do not correlate well with archaeological phase areas, but several sources mention confederations of towns under a single leader both on the coast and in the highlands. This, together with marked differences in status revealed by the burial pattern, suggests that some if not all of the archaeological phase areas may have been integrated politically on a temporary basis at least.

Fig. 36

As was the case during the Regional Developmental Period, the late phases represent different degrees of elaboration in material culture and sociopolitical organization. The three coastal phases occupy larger areas than the three highland ones, a difference that can be attributed in part to the greater severity of geographical barriers in the highlands. Sociopolitical organization sufficiently elaborate to overcome these barriers was achieved only by the Inca, who perfected their techniques during valley by valley conquest of the highlands and coast of Peru.

THE MANTEÑO PHASE

The lands of the Manteño extended along the coast from a little north of the Bahía de Caráquez to the island of Puná, and inland over the Cerro de Hojas and neighbouring hills of southern Manabí. The early Spanish described this region as fertile and yielding good crops of maize, yuca (sweet manioc), beans, potatoes, *aji* (hot pepper), 'and many other roots which

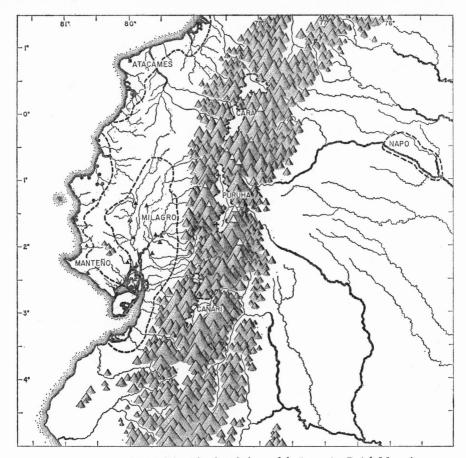

Fig. 36. Geographical distribution of the archaeological phases of the Integration Period. Mountains occupy the area above 1000 metres elevation. Symbols have the following meanings: Cross: Inca administrative centre; Triangle: Huancavilca town at the time of the conquest; Circle: Manteño town at the time of the Conquest; Square: First town seen by the Spanish south of Panama

are useful for the support of man'. Guavas, avocados, pine‑apples and cactus fruits were also plentiful. Guinea‑pigs and a large duck were raised in the houses. Peccaries, deer and other game were hunted, and fishing was important. Honey was collected in the forests. Women did the planting with metal

123

tools, while men engaged in fishing, hunting and trading activities. Maize was ground on flat stone *metates* and made into
tortillas, while fish was often eaten raw. Small pottery pestles
may have been used to crush pepper.

One criterion of technological advance is the modification of
the natural landscape to suit human needs, and in this respect
the Manteño went farther than other prehistoric Ecuadorians.
The growing population placed a burden on natural water
sources, rivers being small and few. Wells were dug throughout southern Manabí, one at the edge of Manta reaching a
depth of 12·8 metres. If the soil was soft, the walls were lined
with uncut stones. Where springs were near the surface or rainfall sufficient, reservoirs were built. Another type of Manteño
construction was the terracing of the ravines and slopes of
Cerro de Hojas and adjacent hills for fields and house sites.
Many of these terraces remain under cultivation today.

The Manteño were the only coastal people to make use of
stone in building. Particularly characteristic are the so-called
'corrales', representing stone foundation walls. At Manta,
where the aboriginal structures have since been destroyed by
modern construction, Saville saw 'the remains of hundreds of
house-sites and mounds covering several square miles'. He
gives a detailed description:

> These houses are often of one room; but there are many with
> two or more, and even up to seven, rooms in one building.
> Little is left of the walls, the bases of which are of rough
> stones set edgewise in the ground. The average width of the
> walls is from 91·4 cm. to 122 cm., the inner and outer part
> being made in the same manner, and probably filled with
> rough stones and earth. . . . Some of the buildings have been
> of enormous size. One was 57·9 m. in length, 11·9 m. in
> width at the southern end, and 11·3 m. at the northern end,
> these being inside measurements. The thickness of the side-

walls was 137 cm., and that of the southern wall 78·7 cm. . . .
The surface of the ground near the northern end of this
large building sloped somewhat towards the sea, and a . . .
graded way was built from the level of the building as an
approach.[1]

Numerous other house foundations occur on the Cerro Bravo
and Cerro de Hojas, indicating a relatively large population
during the late period on this part of the coast. Buildings of
wood or cane roofed with thatch were arranged along streets in
an orderly manner. Temple entrances faced eastward and were
curtained with a cotton tapestry.

Low rectanguloid mounds were interspersed among the
houses. Two on Cerro Jaboncillo, partially excavated by
Saville, contained scattered burials of children and adults,
singly or in groups. Some skeletons had numerous associated
objects, others few, suggesting differences in status. In other
parts of the Manteño area, burial was primary, in the earth rather
than in a mound, or secondary in an urn. Shaft tombs have been
found in several places and their relative rarity suggests they
may have been constructed for individuals of high rank.

At the northern edge of the Manteño Phase area, several interesting customs are reported by chroniclers that cannot be
verified archaeologically. Here, the remains of the dead are said
to have been preserved by flaying the bodies, burning the flesh
and dressing the skins, which were stuffed with straw and hung
with arms outstretched from the temple roof. Heads were
reduced in size to that of a newborn child by a process still employed by the Jivaro Indians of the eastern lowlands, and kept
in chests in the temples, where they were said by the Indians to
remain in good condition for two or three lifetimes.

If the Bahía Phase was the leader in the production of ceremonial objects of stone during the Regional Developmental
Period, the tradition was carried much farther by the Manteño.

Plate 64

Human figures, birds, animals, short semi-cylindrical columns, flat stelae and stools are the most common objects. The stools, with a U-shaped seat resting on an animal or crouching human figure, have been found only on the summits of the Manabí hills, suggesting that they were occupied by civil or religious leaders during deliberations or ceremonies. The carved slabs or

Fig. 37

bas-reliefs all come from Cerro Jaboncillo. Size is difficult to reconstruct since few are complete, but one example measures one metre high, 41·6 cm. wide at the top, 24·9 cm. wide at the bottom and 5·1 to 7·0 cm. thick. The upper end of one surface is dominated by a human or animal figure with the legs and arms bent to each side. The head often fits into a niche in an ornamental frieze with a repetitive geometric pattern. A pair of birds, disks or monkeys often accompanies the principal figure. Stone figures resemble hollow pottery ones in style. A typical

Plate 65

stone receptacle is a square-bodied cat with short legs and a curled tail, always depicted with bared teeth.

According to Cieza de Leon, 'no people in all Peru were so addicted to sacrifices and religious rites',[2] as those of the Manabí coast. Idols were housed in temples and served by priests, who performed ceremonies at stated times. Sweet-smelling wood was burned before the images, and their intervention was sought through prayers, gifts and sacrifices. Cieza thus describes the sacrifice of prisoners of war:

> . . . they assembled and, after having got drunk with their wine, and also having made the prisoner drunk, the chief priest killed him with lancets of stone or copper. They then cut off his head, and offered it, with the body.[3]

In addition to the public temples, each house had its shrine, which held images appropriate to the occupation of the owner. Fishermen had sharks, hunters had animals representing their specialities, etc. Birds, which are depicted on the stone bas-reliefs and shown with figurines, may have been used for

Fig. 37. Manteño Phase stone stela or bas-relief from Cerro Jaboncillo. Height 1 metre.

divination as they were on the north coast of Peru. Pilgrimages were made from all over the interior to Manta, where a giant emerald with supernatural properties was publicly displayed on certain days. Gifts, sacrifices and prayers were made to it by persons who wished to be cured of sickness, and it was so venerated that no Indian would ever reveal its location to the Spaniards even when threatened with death.

In dress, the Manteño followed the style of the Guangala Phase rather than that of the Bahía Phase. Males were generally nude below the waist, a fashion that scandalized the conquistadors, who complained that the brief shirts left exposed what ought to be concealed. Women wore short cotton skirts. Both sexes cut their hair short and wore nose and earrings as well as necklaces of very small gold beads. Lip ornaments and small studs in the cheek at each side of the mouth are also occasionally shown on figurines. Multiple strings of beads, made of silver, gold, turquoise and coloured shells, were worn by men on the arms and legs. Ear ornaments seem to have been less elaborate than in the preceding period, but include similar kinds of 'napkin-rings', solid or perforated beads, and simple rings and pendants. Rather than in the lobe or helix, the ornament was often attached to the inner rim of the ear. Chiefs wore diadems of gold. Men are reported to have had their faces painted or tattooed, the decoration extending from the root of the ear to the chin and varying in width according to preference. Skulls were given a broad high shape by binding the heads of new-born infants between two boards, which were removed at the age of four or five years.

Textiles were produced in abundance and exported. Spindle whorls, which occur by the thousands, are ornamented with excised repeating patterns of birds, animals, faces and geometric motifs. Small and beautifully symmetrical, they resemble those from late cultures of the Peruvian coast. Bone awls and copper needles also occur. Flat and cylindrical pottery stamps, with geometric patterns more reminiscent of Guangala Phase examples than those of the Bahía and Jama-Coaque Phases, may have been used for decoration of textiles. No traces survive of blankets, shawls, shirts and other garments with bird, animal, fish and tree designs in brilliant scarlet, crimson, blue, yellow and other colours, described by the Spanish explorers.

Few metal objects have come from Manteño sites, although the chroniclers mention crowns and diadems, belts, bracelets, leggings, pectorals, tweezers, bells, cups and containers of gold and silver. Minute gold beads were worn by all the coastal people and their delicacy amazed professional Spanish gold-smiths. Pottery moulds for the manufacture of stemmed axes, tanged knives and celts have been found on the Santa Elena

Peninsula. A copper digging-stick point and a broader spade-like implement correspond to the agricultural tools mentioned by the Spanish. Both the working of silver and the technique of casting are additions to the metallurgical technology represented at La Tolita. A small steelyard was used for weighing gold, an indication that standards of value for this commodity at least were rather fixed.

Figurines are either hand-made or mould-made and relatively standardized. The surface is often semi-polished and is usually black. Both sexes are represented. Hand-made examples are large and often lack both clothing and ornament on the body. In appearance, they resemble carved stone figures. The majority are standing, but some are seated on stools similar to the stone seats. Mould-made figurines are small, and detail is restricted to the front side. A wide collar usually made of graduated strands with a large pendant or bib-like projection reaching to the waist corresponds to the Spanish description of male dress, leaving the lower body nude. Bracelets are typical and anklets occasionally worn. On female figurines, a long double-strand necklace or diagonal band replaces the collar and the lower body is also nude. The head-dress tends to be simple, often resembling a smooth helmet. Eye treatment differs from that of earlier figurine styles, a punctate pupil being characteristic.

The pottery of the Manteño Phase is distinctive, emphasizing burnished decoration in lines or bands of polished black which contrast with the lighter grey of the unpolished surface. Anthropomorphic vessels take several forms, among them large jars with a grotesque mask appliquéd on the neck, bottles with the neck in the form of a human head and a small opening at the top providing access to the interior, and vessels with the upper portion in the form of a human or animal figure. One of the latter shows a reclining person eating from a compotera, which is another common vessel shape. Zoomorphic forms include birds as well as animals. Realistically modelled cats

Plate 63

Plate 61
Plate 62

Fig. 38

Plate 59

129

Plate 56

Plate 57

Plate 60

occupy the base of some cylindrical goblets, while others have a small annular base and horizontally fluted walls. Dentate stamping and punctation in zones bounded by incised lines occur in the early part of the phase, as does ornamentation produced with a stamp or mould. Incision and excision are techniques most often represented on spindle whorls, but also employed for beautiful patterns on well-polished vessel surfaces.

Pedestal bases are characteristic, ranging from a low ring on large jars to a slender tall column flaring gracefully at the bottom and supporting a shallow bowl. Both bowls and jars often have composite profiles, with several angular tiers joined by straight or curved surfaces. Jars often become globular above the neck constriction or have a cambered rim profile. Grater bowls have either punctate interiors or shallow parallel grooves.

The Manteño continued the seafaring tradition begun during the Bahía Phase, employing for this purpose large rafts. One captured by Bartolomé Ruiz, who lead a scouting party on Pizarro's first expedition, has been described in detail :

> This vessel . . . had a capacity of up to 30 tons and was constructed of canes as thick as posts, joined with ropes of henequen. The deck was made of thinner canes fastened with the same kind of ropes, and on it were placed passengers and merchandise because the lower part was awash. Masts and lateen yards were made of fine wood and sails of cotton as on our ships, with very good rigging of henequen rope and stones for anchors in the form of millstones.[4]

Such rafts plied the coast of Ecuador, and probably reached much farther northward. The balsa logs, mistaken for canes, gave a buoyancy and stability that made the craft practically unsinkable as long as it remained intact. Smaller fishing rafts may have resembled those used on the southern Guayas coast today.

Plate 58

Differences in status and rank were manifested in differences in the size of houses and in the amount and kind of personal

Fig. 38. Manteño Phase vessel showing a reclining human figure eating from a tall compotera. The surface is polished black. The orifice is in the top of the head

ornament. Puná was administered by seven secondary chiefs under a supreme chief, who was greatly feared and much respected by his subjects, and a parallel situation probably existed on the central Manabí coast with the capital at Manta. The great chief of Puná was surrounded by pomp and escorted by trumpeters and drummers whenever he left his residence. His wives were guarded by eunuchs, whose noses and lips were also cut off to make them physically unattractive. Religion was formalized and public temples were tended by priests. Occupational specialization must have existed in arts and crafts also. Order and justice prevailed, according to the Spaniards, and towns were well laid out and maintained.

THE MILAGRO PHASE

Between the foot of the Andes and the coastal hills, in the region occupied earlier by the Daule and Tejar Phases, a late culture developed that differed in most archaeologically observable respects from that of the Manteño seafarers. Sites are distributed over a larger area than that occupied by any other phase, ex-tending from the Quevedo region southward to the Peruvian border, and representing what is probably the culmination of a gradual territorial expansion.

Although hunting and fishing were still practised, agricul-ture was the primary subsistence resource. In forested parts of the area, fields were cleared and the brush burned to prepare the land for planting. Where rainy-season flooding occurred, forest growth was inhibited and planting could be done with a dig-ging stick as soon as the water subsided. Weeding kept out grass. Maize and lima beans were the most prolific crops, with twenty- to forty-fold returns. Sweet potatoes, yuca (sweet manioc) and other varieties of beans, were also grown.

A considerable population density is implied by the abun-dance of Milagro Phase sites. Artificial mounds occur by the hundreds, being especially numerous in the southern Guayas basin, where the land is inundated every year for several months during the rainy season. Mound building may have been stimu-lated by a desire to increase the amount of solid ground, but evidence that it was not simply a practical measure is provided by the presence of mounds in areas where flooding does not occur and by the impressive height of some of the construc-tions, far exceeding the requirements of high water level.

Around Milagro, both habitation sites and burial mounds are numerous. A few groups of unusually large mounds may represent centres of administrative or religious activity, or both. Closer to the Río Babahoyo, large numbers of small low house platforms surround several much larger platform and cemetery mounds. Platform mounds up to 100 metres long, 30 metres wide and 10 metres high loom impressively over the generally flat terrain. Several have been cut into by treasure hunters, showing that they do not contain burial urns. This, added to

Plate 41

132

their large size, makes a ceremonial function seem a safe guess. Houses had walls of poles and flattened cane with gabled thatched roofs, a type of construction still commonly used on the southern coast.

Burial was in artificial mounds, which differ considerably both in size and in the number and arrangements of urns. Larger mounds often contain a variety of burials, including direct interments, urns covered by a single inverted jar, and the remarkable 'chimney' urns, composed of a series of jars with the bottoms knocked out placed one above the other to produce a tube nearly 5 metres high. Pottery and metal objects of many kinds were placed with the dead. In addition, the protection afforded by the urns and the preservative coating created by copper corrosion has occasionally allowed preservation of basketry, textiles, cordage and wood. Since little besides pottery is found in habitation refuse, these grave lots immensely enlarge the inventory of material culture in addition to shedding considerable light on burial practices.

Plate 42

The burial goods vary widely in quantity and kind, but three general categories can be distinguished. At one end of the range are burials with relatively few items: 4 pottery vessels, or 6 pots and a copper knife, or 5 pots, a needle and a ring, or 2 pots, 8 earrings and a few beads. Burials in this category may occur either directly in the ground, in a single urn, at the bottom of a chimney, or in the chimney tube, and probably represent individuals relatively low in the social hierarchy. At the opposite extreme are rare burials accompanied not only by a great quantity of gold, silver and copper rings, earrings, nose-rings, beads, bells, tweezers, knives and needles, but also a number of unusual items indicative of prestige. Among the latter are gilded collars with embossed designs, pyrite mirrors framed in silver, heavy copper plaques with a stylized human face, crowns with silver feathers, garments covered with silver pendants, *atlatls* with a carved wooden handle and a copper hook,

and silver bowls. A person so honoured must have been of outstanding rank, perhaps an important chief.

Between these two extremes is an intermediate category, into
which the majority of the urn burials fall. Certain kinds of objects are almost always included, such as pottery vessels, copper
rings of several sizes, copper or gilt-copper nose-rings, copper-
tweezers, copper or silver earrings often with pendants, pottery
spindle whorls, small copper bells, and various kinds of beads.
While most objects occur singly or in a frequency less than five
in a single urn, the number of pottery vessels may reach 20, and
copper rings may total over 100. It is probable that differences
of this nature are correlated with differences in sex and occupation of the deceased.

Although realistic figurines do not exist, some details of
dress and ornament can be reconstructed from the grave goods
and early Spanish descriptions. Men wore a cotton loin-cloth,
arranged so that the end hung down the back almost to the
ground, while women wore a skirt reaching to the knees. Both
might also wear a sleeveless shirt. Some of these textiles had
warp-float designs, or were dyed by the *ikat* process, in which
fine patterns were produced by dyeing parts of the threads by a
resist technique before weaving. Garments of chiefs were embellished by the attachment of many small silver plates, which
must have glittered in the sun.

Ear and nose ornaments are graceful and elegant in design. A
single piece of wire, with round, oval, rectanguloid or diamond-
shaped cross-section, was bent into a series of loops and coils,
and then flattened at the upper end to produce a hollow ring for
insertion into a perforation in the ear. The discovery of a dozen
identical ornaments of gold wire in one burial urn suggests that
they were attached six on each side along the outer edge of the
ear. More elaborate ear ornaments generally occur in pairs, indicating that they were probably suspended from the lobe. One
of the most attractive consists of two cascades of loops terminat-

Plate 51

Plate 52

Fig. 39a, b, e

Plate 50

Fig. 39e

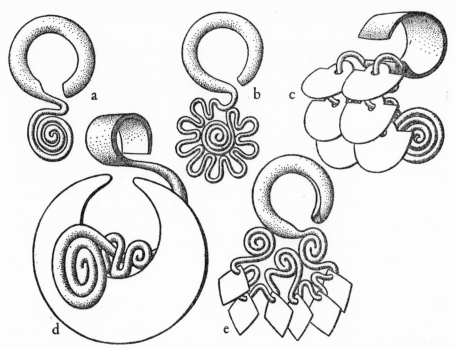

Fig. 39. Typical Milagro Phase silver earrings. a. Hollow ring with a single pendant coil; b. Hollow ring with an elaborate pendant coil; c. Flat ring with double cascade of loops ending in coils each with three gold dangles; d. Flat ring with pendant coil and large semi-lunar dangle; e. Hollow ring with a series of pendant coils and diamond-shaped dangles.

ing in a coil, with a small gold pendant hanging from each loop. Others have a single large loop and a large gold or silver dangle.

    Two general types of nose-rings are typical. The commonest is a solid copper ring, often gilded, weighing 14 to 114 gr. Cross-section is circular or diamond-shaped. From one to 13 such rings may occur in a single burial urn of the intermediate category. Much rarer are silver or gold nose ornaments produced by joining two coils of flattened wire. More elaborate constructions have multiple small coils, each with a dangle attached at the centre by a cotter. A single wire may change

Fig. 39d

Fig. 40a

Fig. 40b

Fig. 40c, d
Fig. 40e

from circular to square cross-section in different parts of the ornament. Gold nose-rings may have at the centre of each coil a flat turquoise bead bordered by minute gold balls.

In the burials, silver beads outnumber those of stone, shell or gold. Several sizes were manufactured from small rectangular pieces of metal by joining the long edges to form a slender tube or the short edges to create a bead of larger diameter. Beads were strung as necklaces or woven into strips of fabric. Small copper bells have two perforations at the top suggesting they were sewed to a garment. Small studs with heads delicately assembled from minute balls may have been worn in the cheeks.

Fig. 41d

Special ornaments worn by persons of high rank include a broad collar of gold or gilded silver with a human face embossed at the centre front, a crown of real plumes enhanced by the

Fig. 40. Varieties of Milagro Phase nose-rings. a. Common solid copper type; b. Common double-coil type, usually executed in silver; c. Silver multiple-coil type with small gold dangles at the centre of each coil; d. Rare silver type with two lateral coils each with a dangle; e. Rare elaboration of the double-coil type from a gold wire 2·72 metres long

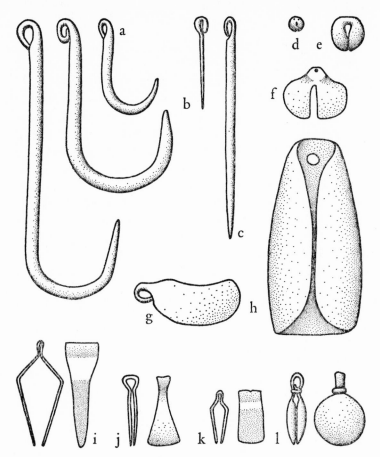

Fig. 41. Small copper objects of Milagro Phase manufacture. a. Fish-hooks; b. Pin with bell-head; c. Needle; d-f. Bells with free pebble clappers; g. Knife; h. Clapperless bell; i-l. Varieties of tweezers

addition of long narrow artificial feathers of silver or gold, large gold disks, wide gold bracelets, and small circular polished pyrite mirrors set in a decorated silver frame. Chiefs also had their upper front incisors perforated for insertion of gold studs. In full regalia, they must have been an impressive sight.

Fig. 41i–l
Fig. 41c

Fig. 41g

Fig. 42d, f

Fig. 42c, e

Fig. 42a, b
Fig. 41a

Fig. 41b

In the Milagro Phase, copper was employed for a variety or tools as well as ornaments. Tweezers with tapered, expanded or circular arms are abundant. Next in frequency are needles, the eye formed by a flattened projection from the broad end, looped over and inserted into the shaft. Except for a small knife with a loop at one end, cutting tools typically have a symmetrical semi-lunar blade with a narrow tang at the centre back for insertion into a wooden handle, or a broader projection perforated for hafting. A rarer type of axe is slightly narrower at the blade than at the butt, which is perforated for attachment to a handle. Cutting tools without either tang or perforation also occur. Less common objects include fish-hooks, with an eye constructed like those of needles, combs, *atlatl* hooks, and pins with small bell heads. No metallurgical analysis has been made of composition and techniques of manufacture, but the extensive use of copper and silver, the addition of casting to techniques represented earlier, and the use of metal for tools as well as for luxury items all indicate considerable advance over the Regional Developmental Period.

One kind of metal object of particular interest because of its resemblance to 'axe money' used in Mexico is a thin copper plate of approximately axe shape, reinforced by a rib around the edge. Up to several hundred have come from a single burial, but they are not common as grave goods, perhaps because their commercial value inhibited their being taken out of circulation. Another object of possible monetary or prestige

Plates 53–55

value is an anthropomorphic copper plaque, which occurs only with burials of individuals whose high status is implied by the other associated objects.

Few archaeological remains shed light on religion. Ovoid lumps of unfired clay with a pair of large breast-like nubbins on one side probably represent crude figurines. Occasional large cones of the same fine clay have no apparent use, suggesting

Plate 49

ritual significance. Amulets of soft whitish stone are carved in

Fig. 42. Milagro Phase copper tool types. a. Chisel; b. Axe with expanding blade; c. Axe with butt perforated for hafting; d, f. Tanged cutting tools; e. Cutting tool with broad tang perforated for hafting

anthropomorphic, frog and snake forms, or combinations of human and animal. Snakes and frogs, as well as birds and human figures, are also the principal elements in relief ornament on small polished bowls with low pedestal bases. Frogs are common symbols of rain in Mesoamerica, and in view of other evidence of Mesoamerican influence may have had similar significance for the Milagro Phase people. Miniature human, bird and animal carvings in stone and bone may have served as amulets.

Plate 45

Plate 48

Milagro Phase pottery is artistically impoverished in comparison to that of the preceding period. Vessels of domestic use, which make up the bulk of the production, are typically thickwalled, with unpolished surfaces. Decoration is restricted to a narrow zone adjacent to the rim on large jars or the upper exterior of tripods, and usually executed by incision or combing. Red painting of the rim continues an ancient tradition, and red

Plate 44

stripes may be applied to jar exteriors. Small jars and bowls often have a polished red slip on the exterior or interior surface. A row of small nubbins may occur on the exterior on slightly carinated forms, or a flange with an undulating edge may be applied. On bowl interiors, the most common decorative technique is burnished lines in very simple radiating patterns. Negative painting is relatively rare, but beautifully executed. Appliqué-decorated polished brown or black bowls and miniature excised vessels are outstanding for symmetry and care of workmanship.

Plate 47
Plate 45

Among typical shapes are the large jars used as burial urns, but probably manufactured for various domestic functions also, to judge from the frequency of sherds in village refuse. The majority are between 50 and 100 cm. in height, with diameters slightly less. The blackened bottoms of many tripod jars indicate that they were used for certain kinds of cooking. Bifurcated straight or twisted legs are characteristic, but loop supports also occur. Bowls have flat bases, out-sloping walls and slightly thickened notched rims. Compoteras vary greatly in size, and often have bases with cut-out ornament. Annular-based bowls of more rounded contour have incised or combed interior treatment, placing them in the category of grater bowls. Two noncontainer forms are stools and drums. In general, forms are not graceful and symmetry is poor.

Plates 43, 44

Plate 46

Diagnostic Manteño anthropomorphic jars frequently occur in Milagro Phase burial urns, verifying the contemporaneity of the two phases and the existence of trade between them. The rare pottery stamps may also be of trade origin. The relatively low agricultural potential of the Manteño Phase region in comparison to the Guayas basin makes it probable that vegetable produce was exchanged for salt, which was one of the principal Manteño surplus items.

At the time of Spanish settlement, the Guayas basin was inhabited by Huancavilca Indians. The distribution of Huan

Fig. 36

cavilca towns coincides so well with that of the Milagro Phase sites that there can be little doubt of continuity, and the correlation is supported by the presence of green glass trade beads in some urn burials. According to the Spaniards, the Huancavilca also inhabited two towns west of the Colonche Hills, in what is archaeologically Manteño territory. Whether this represents a late expansion westward or an error in reporting is uncertain.

THE ATACAMES PHASE

South of Panama, the first well-peopled area encountered by Pizarro was around Atacames, on the Esmeraldas coast. Here, 10,000 warriors received the 80 Spaniards. Although the reception was cordial, the Spaniards felt themselves uncomfortably outnumbered and retreated to await reinforcements before continuing down the coast. Jerez describes Atacames as composed of more than 3000 houses, which were arranged in an orderly manner along streets and plazas. Sámanos reports 1500 houses, but adds that there were other towns near by, which may be included in the larger estimate.

Large habitation sites, consisting of shallow deposits of plain sherds several kilometres long, exist not only in the Atacames region, but at various other places along the coast as far as the Colombian border. Mounds also occur, some measuring 20 metres in diameter and 4 metres high. In a few cases, as at La Tolita, they contain abundant sherds and other kinds of refuse, but this seems to be an accidental result of collecting the dirt from areas of previous habitation. Urn and chimney burials were sometimes placed in mounds, and at other times directly in the ground. The urn contents are poorly described, but one interesting feature is the presence of gold inlay in the teeth. One individual had inlay not only in the four upper incisors, but also in the canines and first pre-molars. Gold studs were also inserted into the skin of the face for ornamental effect.

Although absence of systematic stratigraphic investigation makes it impossible to differentiate with any degree of confidence between artifacts of this period and those of the earlier Tolita Phase, the predominance of plain sherds in the village refuse indicates a decline in frequency of decoration and variety of vessel shape paralleling that to the south. Flat-bottomed bowls and annular-based jars probably belong to the Integration Period here as elsewhere. One artifact that appears to be diagnostic is a large flat spindle whorl with a small conical projection at the upper centre through which the perforation runs.

A number of factors make the Esmeraldas coast potentially important archaeologically. A carbon-14 date of AD 270 from a chimney burial at La Tolita suggests that the practice may be earlier here than in the Guayas basin. Tooth inlay and platform mound construction also link the two areas. Although the coast east of the Río Esmeraldas was reported by Pizarro to be sparsely inhabited, a Manteño-like anthropomorphic vessel from La Tolita indicates that this site continued to be occupied until a relatively late time. If withdrawal subsequently occurred, this trend is the opposite of what is evident to the south, and understanding of its causes becomes a significant problem.

THE CARA PHASE

Lacunae in the archaeological data make it difficult to describe the late cultures of the Ibarra and Quito basins. Except for complexes of circular earth-walled houses or *bohíos* at the northern margin of the area, information comes almost entirely from burials. Several kinds are reported, with differences in elaborateness of construction and type of grave goods that may reflect temporal, areal or status differences, or all three. Some of the generally accepted chronological distinctions in the north highlands seem instead to represent differences between domestic and burial aspects of the same culture, or minor geographical variations in frequency of different kinds of pottery decoration. Using the coastal chronology as a guide, most of the archaeological remains fit best into the Integration Period.

Sites are concentrated below the 3000 metre contour, and usually occupy the margins of rivers. Subsistence was based on farming, with maize, potatoes and quinoa the principal crops. Quinoa seeds were made into a drink or cooked and eaten like rice. Guineapigs and llamas were domesticated, and deer, rabbits, and various game birds were hunted. Cotton was raised in quantity for textile production.

The central portion of the area, south of the Río Chonta and northeast of the Río Guayllabamba, contains many platform mounds singly or in groups. One of the largest measures 120 by 150 metres at the base, 75 by 95 metres at the platform, and is 40 metres high. Some have a long earthen ramp at the centre of one long side, which usually ends at the edge of a creek. In outline they may be circular or elliptical as well as rectanguloid. Few sherds or artifacts are associated with the large mounds, a situation usually indicative of ceremonial or administrative use. Layers of burned earth suggest successive building stages in some structures. In others, construction of lumps of adobe has been observed. Smaller mounds often contain a few burials or are built over burial pits.

The dominant pattern of burial was in a pit excavated in the house floor. Simple pits vary between 35 cm. and 1·5 metres in diameter and between 1 and 2 metres in depth. The majority contain a single individual, but multiple occupants have been reported. Also common are shafts with a niche or chamber cut into the side at the bottom, in which the burial was often placed. Offerings generally take the form of from one to eight pottery vessels, sometimes interred part of the way up the shaft rather than beside the skeleton. Metal objects are rare, a reflection of their general scarcity in the artifact inventory. Deer bones represent food to sustain the deceased in the afterworld.

Contrasting with these simple tombs are elaborate multiple-chambered structures. Their concentration on slopes at the north-eastern limit of the Cara Phase region suggests that this may have been a place reserved for burial of high-ranking persons. Tombs at El Angel and Huaca, described by Verneau and Rivet, contain multiple burials arranged so as to suggest they represent a chief and wives or retainers. Variations include a single pit with up to six radiating chambers at the same depth or at different depths, a single pit with a chamber at the bottom containing one skeleton and additional skeletons stratified in the shaft between layers of stones and dirt, and multiple pits with chambers connected by tunnels to a central pit with the principal burial, which had the richest grave goods.

Fig. 43

Little can be said about religious practices. According to tradition, the Cara worshipped the sky and the snow-capped peaks, to which they made pilgrimages led by priests to offer sacrifices. Stone and wooden idols were also entreated with offerings of maize, chicha and coca. War prisoners were used when the occasion required human sacrifice, their still-beating hearts torn out and presented to the waiting gods.

Fig. 44a–c

Stone artifacts include celts and several forms of axes with grooves, 'ears', or a perforation for hafting. These and disk or star club heads assume shapes often executed in copper to the south and on the coast. Other common stone objects include *atlatl* hooks and labrets.

Fig. 44d–f

Copper is rare and used principally for ornaments, such as pins, rings, nose-rings and small bells. Occasional axes and star club heads may have been acquired by trade from the south rather than locally manufactured. Gold disks and pectorals perforated for attachment to a necklace or garment are more like ornaments from Colombia than contemporary Ecuadorian products from other areas.

A characteristic pottery artifact is a trumpet modelled in the form of a shell and ornamented with incised or painted decor-

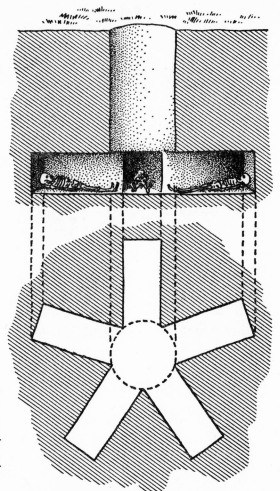

Fig. 43. Pit tomb with five radiating chambers, one of the complex forms at the cemetery of Huaca on the northern slopes of the Ibarra basin

ation, perhaps a pottery substitute for the shell trumpets used on the coast. Bone flutes are another common musical instrument. Figurines are rare and crude. Small pottery masks are uncommon. Spindle whorls were fashioned from sherds.

Pottery decoration is principally by negative painting combined with red bands, which often divide the design into zones.

Fig. 45

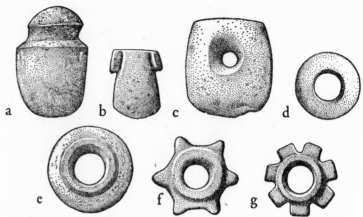

a   b   c   d

e   f   g

*Fig. 44. Types of stone axe and club heads from the Cara Phase. a. Grooved axe;
b. 'Eared' axe; c. Perforated axe; d-e. Disk club; f. Star club*

Plate 68

Plate 67

Fig. 46

Either red bands or negative painting are also used independently on a plain or white-slipped surface. Small polished jars
may have a row of nubbins around the shoulder or anthropomorphic or zoomorphic appliqué, but the vessel is rarely dis-
torted from its circular form. In addition to the tall tripod jars
with solid conical legs, annular-based jars with flaring rims,
compoteras and annular-based bowls diagnostic of the Integra-

*Fig. 45. Interiors of pedestal bowls of the Cara Phase with negative (black) and red (stippled) painted decora-
tion*

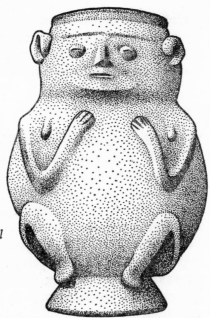

*Fig. 46. Anthropomorphic jar from El
Angel, Carchi Province*

tion Period throughout Ecuador, there are several local forms.
One is a tall slender jar with an ovoid body and a long cylindrical neck, usually with painted decoration. Another is a
small jar with an angular shoulder and a slightly constricted,
collar-like rim often with two small handles at opposite sides.
Shoe-shaped vessels are more common than in other Ecuadorian regions, perhaps a reflection of Colombian influence.

Plate 66

The archaeological evidence, particularly the large artificial
mounds and marked differential treatment of the dead, suggests
that social stratification set apart a small group of élite from the
mass of the populace. According to oral traditions recorded by
the early Spaniards, chiefs exercised absolute power and frequently waged war against each other. At the time of the Inca
conquest, the ruler of Cayambe is said to have held sovereignty
over most of the Quito and Ibarra basins, perhaps leader of a

confederation of autonomous city-states for mutual defence against a common enemy. Resistance was sufficiently effective to hold off the Inca for 17 years and defeat finally came only a few decades before the Spanish Conquest.

THE PURUHÁ PHASE

Most of the information on the Riobamba basin derives from the work of Jacinto Jijón y Caamaño, who suggested a sequence of several periods based on differences in pottery shape and decoration. His inferences have not been verified by stratigraphic excavation, and the chronology differs so markedly from that on the central coast as to cast doubt on its accuracy. Proto-Panzaleo I and II, supposedly the earliest periods, correspond in many details of pottery decoration and shape to the most recent coastal complex, the Milagro Phase. San Sebastián, Elenpata and Huavalac seem to label differences in pottery types from cemetery and habitation sites belonging to the same general group. Pending detailed investigation, all remains not clearly assignable to the Tuncahuán Phase have therefore been incorporated into a late occupation, named after the inhabitants at the time of contact, the Puruhá.

The great snow-capped peak of Chimborazo divides the high central basin into northern and southern halves, each drained by a tributary of the Río Pastaza, which flows eastward into the Amazonian forests. Although tradition assigns the north to the Latacunga and the south to the Puruhá, archaeological differences are not pronounced. Habitation sites, located below the 3000 metre contour, contain remnants of dry stone walls, cobbles set in mud mortar, or *tapia* (puddled clay), either alone or faced on the exterior with stone. At Guano, Jijón describes a wall 3·6 metres high constructed of thin quadrangular stones laid with mud mortar in horizontal rows. The site area was estimated at 100,000 square metres. Maize and llama remains were encountered during excavation of the room refuse, along with potsherds and grinding stones.

The burial pattern resembles that to the north, differing principally in the greater amount of grave goods typically associated and the absence of the most elaborate multiple tombs. Pits were excavated 80 cm. to 1·30 metres in diameter and 50 cm. to 1·80 metres deep, sometimes with a chamber cut into the side at the bottom. Typically, the chamber was stepped down below the base of the shaft. Tombs contained a single individual, whether adult or child, in a tightly flexed position. Two to eight pottery vessels, including tripod jars and bowls, and annular-based bowls (the latter often serving as lids for the jars), occurred with all burials. Rare additional objects included shell beads, grinding stones and *manos*. In 57 burial pits excavated, no metal was found, though copper rings, pins, shawl pins (*tupus*) and an axe with a perforated tang have been collected in the vicinity.

Religious practices are poorly known. Chimborazo and Tungurahua, the tallest snow-clad peaks, are said to have embodied two deities, the former male and the latter female, from which the Puruhá were descended. On Chimborazo, a temple stood at the edge of the eternal snow. Offerings were brought from throughout the region, and llamas or young virgins of high rank were sacrificed on certain occasions.

Artifacts of stone are not abundant, and include the same varieties of celts, axes, club heads and *atlatl* hooks found elsewhere in the highlands. Crude pottery figurines are mentioned in the literature but not described, and other kinds of pottery artifacts are not reported. Metal tools and ornaments are rare, although some anthropomorphic vessels have ears perforated for insertion of ornaments along the outer edge. Nose-rings, so typical of the coast, are not depicted. Cactus fibre was used for making sandals, and fine textiles were woven from cotton and wool.

Fig. 47. Anthropomorphic jars from the Puruhá Phase cemetery of Elen-pata, Riobamba basin, with negative painted decoration

The pottery, although incorporating numerous highland features, bears a striking resemblance to that of the Milagro Phase at the foot of the mountains to the west. Combed decoration on jar necks and bowl interiors is identical in tech-nique and motif in the two phases. Negative painting in dots and stripes on a plain or red-slipped surface, and incised pat-terns on an unpolished surface are also common in both areas. Shared vessel shapes include compoteras, often with cut-out decoration of the pedestal base, globular jars with short necks, tripod jars with bifurcated or twisted legs, and grater bowls, the interior roughened by combed bands. The most distinctive Puruhá Phase vessels are anthropomorphic jars. One type has a highly stylized face on each side of the out-slanting neck and negative painting with red bands on the body; another is plain or incised and has a stylized human face on one side. A local variety of tripod has legs of flattened strips referred to as *hoja de*

Plate 74

Plate 71

Plate 69
Fig. 47

Plate 71

cabuya because of their resemblance to leaves of the agave plant. Small bowls with incised designs of slanting parallel lines have a handle on one side at the rim.

Information on sociopolitical organization comes from oral traditions. The Puruhá nation included a large number of tribes, each with a chief, over which reigned a supreme chief. The status of this individual was such that he possessed as a private retreat near the capital a region of small lakes connected by artificial canals and surrounded by wooded hills on which buildings were located. The Puruhá were constantly at war with their neighbours, employing lances, wooden swords, and slings with pellets of heavy wood, which they flung with accuracy equalling that of a rifle bullet. After the Inca conquest in the latter part of the fifteenth century, the earlier culture was broken down by colonists with different traditions imported from southern Peru, and by resident administrators who organized the society along Inca lines.

THE CAÑARI PHASE

As of present knowledge, the most highly developed cultural phase in the highlands was that occupying the Cuenca, Cañar and Alausí basins of the south. This could be a result of more favourable environmental conditions, a longer tradition of settled life, greater accessibility to influences from the south and west; or the impression of a higher cultural level in these areas may have mistakenly arisen simply because there is more surviving evidence from them. Habitation sites are numerous, located as in other basins below the 3000 metre contour where favourable agricultural land occurs. Many are small, suggesting a settlement pattern of hamlets scattered among the fields. The climatic range allowed a wide variety of the cultivated plants known aboriginally to be grown. In the warmer lower valleys of the Alausí and Jubones rivers, enough coca was raised to supply the entire province. Although llamas, guanacos and guinea-pigs were domesticated, fishing and hunting continued to supplement the diet.

The Cuenca basin is famous for a large number of rich graves, discovered and destroyed by treasure hunters. Circular or square pit-tombs occur in small groups or large cemeteries. The circular type may have a chamber. Depth is from very shallow to 4 metres. Chambers may be closed off with a wall of stones or sticks, and the pit fill often has alternating layers of stone and earth. Tombs of high-ranking individuals are incredibly rich. Some at Sigsig and Ucur produced between 100 and 200 kg. of gold disks, nose-rings, bracelets, earrings, bells, crowns, shield coverings, flutes, and bowls of various sizes. Cylindrical vessels and belts combined gold and silver in two-tone patterns. Many objects were decorated with embossed figures. Such burials contrast markedly with those of lesser individuals, which contain few or no associated artifacts.

The Cañari religion focused on natural objects such as trees, rocks, the sky, volcanoes and other mountains, river confluences and lakes. A cave on the summit of Curitaqui, near the centre of the Cuenca basin, was the scene each year of the sacrifice of 100 young children to ensure a bountiful harvest. Highly respected priests served as intermediaries between the people and the gods.

The Cañari not only produced an abundance of gold objects from the readily available alluvial supply, but seem to be the only group to rival the Milagro Phase in the use of copper for tools. Forms are similar, including axes with parallel or convex sides and a perforation for hafting, knives with curved blade and narrow tang, star club heads and needles. Rings, broad-headed pins and artificial feathers are among copper ornaments.

Stone tools are also abundant, and represent the same types of axes and club heads found to the north. *Atlatl* hooks em-

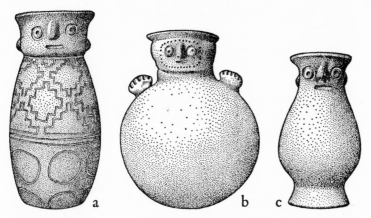

*Fig. 48. Anthropomorphic jars of the Cañari Phase. a. Cylindrical jar with incised de,
coration on the body; b. Flattened canteen,shaped jar; c. Annular,based jar.*

phasize bird,headed outlines. Serpentine and turquoise beads
continue to be made for ornament. Preservation has restricted
evidence of wood,working to a few spear,thrower (*atlatl*) shafts,
whose carved decoration resembles that on Milagro Phase ex,
amples. Textiles are described by the first Spaniards, and their
presence in a grave at Sigsig is implied by numerous thin
circular gold and silver pendants similar to those sewed on to
garments on the coast. Small gold tubes may have ornamented
a fringe.

Decorated pottery is characterized by thin walls and polished
surfaces, a heritage from the preceding Chaullabamba Phase.
Azógues was renowned in the colonial period for pottery,
making because of the fine quality of the local clay. The pre,
dominance of relatively thick plain sherds in habitation sites
parallels the situation in late period sites elsewhere. A local
specialization is a cylindroid jar, often with an anthropomor,   *Fig. 48a, c*
phic face near the rim on one side. Eyes take the form of a ring
with a central punctation, the mouth is a narrow incision and
the nose is modelled in relief. Ears may be shown as low pro,

Fig. 48b

Fig. 48a, c

cf. Plates 53-55

jections. Hands rising at the shoulder are rare and delineation of lower limbs rarer still. Decoration is by red bands, negative painting, fine incision on a polished surface, or incision separating redandbuff or redandblack zones. Annularbased and flatbottomed jars, compoteras, and anthropomorphic vessels are forms shared with other Integration Period complexes.

Trade relations with neighbouring groups are reflected in a number of objects of foreign origin. Several Chimú stirrupspout jars have been found in the Cuenca basin, implying communication with the north Peruvian coast. Milagro Phase artifacts include a carved stone amulet from Ingapirca and a copper anthropomorphic plaque of the 'status symbol' type from Azógues. Bifurcated and *hoja de cabuya* tripod legs and rimhandle bowls, diagnostic Puruhá Phase forms, have come from sites in the Cañar basin.

Although the differential treatment of the dead suggests advanced social stratification, tradition describes the Cañari as divided into a number of warring tribes, each with its chief. This lack of centralization of authority may in part account for the slight resistance initially offered to the advancing Inca army. Subsequently, the Cañari revolted, but unsuccessfully. The Inca punishment was severe: 8000 prisoners were killed, in addition to old people of both sexes, and many of the survivors were moved to Cuzco. The village of Cojitambo was repopulated completely by Indians from Cuzco. Once secured, the beauty and agreeable climate of the Cuenca basin made it the favourite residence of Topa Inca and his son Huayna Capac, who was born at the palace of Tomebamba.

THE NAPO PHASE

The eastern Andean slopes and lowlands are almost unknown archaeologically. Sites appear to be most numerous adjacent to the Quito and Ibarra basins in the north and the Cuenca basin in the south. The majority are late and may in part re-present colonies that specialized in the raising of tropical crops of commercial value, such as coca. With decreasing elevation, conditions favouring agriculture diminish and so does evidence of settled life. When Orellana made the first exploratory voyage down the Napo to the Amazon in 1542, he found no Indian villages in what is now Ecuadorian territory.

For a brief period between AD 1100 and 1200, the banks of the Napo high enough to escape rainy-season flooding were occupied by people with a distinctive ceramic complex. Villages composed of a single or double row of houses stretched along the bank for some 600 metres, but the superficial depth of the sherd refuse indicates that they were occupied for a rather short time. Burial was in anthropomorphic urns, apparently interred at random or beneath house floors rather than in cemeteries. No grave offerings are reported.

Apart from pottery, few artifacts are known to be associated with the Napo Phase. Large roller stamps with deeply excised surfaces have a small handle at each end like a rolling-pin. Stone axes take typical highland forms. No figurines, whistles, stools or other pottery objects have been reported.

The ceramic complex includes a variety of decorative techniques, sometimes in intricate combinations. Most frequent is painting, either red-on-white, black-on-white or polychrome *Plates 73, 75, 76* (red and black on white). The art style combines angles and curves into attractive over-all designs, often giving the effect of negative painting. True negative painting is very rare. Incision takes a variety of forms, executed by single or double pointed or blunt-ended tools. Design areas composed of broad grooves were white-slipped, and the grooves subsequently painted red or outlined by polychrome. Excision was often combined with *Plate 74* incision. In the most complicated type, excised portions of a red-slipped surface were filled with white pigment. Appliqué *Plate 72* was used only for anthropomorphic detail on jars. Typical

Plate 75

vessel shapes include large broad-rimmed basins, bowls with pronounced carination, shallow annular-based bowls, and deep flat-bottomed jars with a curved cambered rim. Most bowls and jars are square.

Resemblances between this complex and known archaeo-logical phases of the Ecuadorian highlands are slight. An Andean origin is nevertheless implied by the presence of white-on-red and negative painting, and cylindrical stamps. Further-more, the general cultural pattern indicates dependence upon more productive agriculture than can be maintained in the tropical forest. It appears that the population abandoned their homeland, perhaps to avoid subjugation by an invading group, and sought refuge in the empty lands east of the Andes. A short period of residence on the Napo sufficed to reveal the poverty of the soil and the scarcity of game and fish, particu-larly during the long period of flooding each year. Moving on in search of better land, some of the population took the course of least resistance down river. Their passage can be traced via the distinctive ceramic style as far as the island of Marajó at the mouth of the Amazon, where they are known in archaeo-logical literature as the Marajoara Phase.

REGIONAL VARIATION DURING THE INTEGRATION
PERIOD

As might be expected from the diversity of the Regional Developmental Period cultures and differences in the environ-ments to which they were adapted, cultural evolution did not proceed at an even rate toward increasing complexity during the late period. The largest territorial expansion was achieved by the Milagro Phase, which occupied the Guayas basin and extended along the foot of the Andes to the modern Peruvian border. Whatever cultural impulses led to this spread were favoured by the absence of abrupt geographical or ecological

Fig. 36

transitions within the area, which would have necessitated drastic modifications in subsistence techniques. Along the shore, the Manteño Phase probably reached its ecological limit, since further expansion to the north, south or inland would have involved adaptation to markedly different conditions of vegetation and rainfall. Stricter environmental limitations existed in the highland basins, and their rigidity is expressed in the near universality of site location below the 3000 metre contour line, the approximate altitude above which agriculture becomes unproductive. Interbasin political unification also may have been inhibited by the circumstances that the two valleys most similar in vegetation and climate are separated by the higher and more arid Riobamba basin, which required different techniques for intensive subsistence exploitation.

The influence of geography can also be discerned in the fact that each highland phase resembles that on the corresponding portion of the coast. The Cara Phase of the Quito and Ibarra basins is more similar in many traits of material culture to the Atacames Phase of the Esmeraldas coast than to the Puruhá Phase, its highland neighbour to the south. The Cañari are comparable to the Manteño of Puná Island, while ceramically at least, the Puruhá Phase of the central highlands is affiliated most closely with the Milagro Phase of the central coast. In each case, rivers draining from the highlands provide a route of access to that part of the coast where the greatest similarities occur. Historical traditions describe relations between most of these highland/lowland pairs as hostile; if so, some of the cultural exchange may have been effected by prisoners spared the sacrificial knife.

Fig. 36

Highland/lowland communication paths intersect in the highlands with influences passing north–south via the intermontane corridor. The Cara Phase reflects Colombian influence in its emphasis on red and negative painted pottery and pit/and/chamber tomb construction, as well as in the style of

gold ornaments and several pottery vessel shapes. These characteristics fade out toward the south, as Peruvian influences become gradually stronger. The presence of Chimú stirrup-spout
jars in the Cuenca basin indicates that the same passes serving
as commercial routes today between the south Ecuadorian highlands and the north Peruvian coast were in use during the
Integration Period.

On the coast, the strong Mesoamerican influence evident in
the material culture of the Regional Developmental Period has
largely disappeared. In the social and religious realm, however,
early Spanish explorers describe a number of Mesoamerican
practices, especially in the Manteño region. Among these are
burning of incense in temples, human sacrifice with the cutting-
out of the victim's heart, flaying of the body, shrinking of
heads, and naming of children after the day of their birth. Some
of these practices are also reported in the north highlands. In all
probability, many are survivals of introductions made during
the Regional Developmental Period. One new element of
Mesoamerican origin, however, can be assigned to the Integration Period: ornamental gold inlay on the front of the upper
incisor teeth.

If pronounced differential treatment of the dead is used as a
criterion, social stratification reached its greatest elaboration in
the Cañari, Cara and Milagro Phases. The Spanish reported
that throughout both highlands and coast, wives and sometimes retainers were buried with important chiefs. In life, they
were treated with deference and respect, and provided with a
formal escort when they appeared in public. Throughout the
area, priests played an important role, leading public ceremonies, communicating with the gods and interpreting their
wishes to the people.

Archaeological evidence does not suggest supremacy of one
phase over the others in level of sociopolitical integration. The
settlement pattern in all regions, as far as it is known, suggests

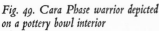
Fig. 49. Cara Phase warrior depicted on a pottery bowl interior

an advanced nuclear centre or city-state organization. The chief and his retainers, priests and various craftsmen probably lived in a town supported by the produce of farmers scattered over the surrounding countryside. The latter came to town to ex-change goods at the market, to participate in festivals, and to offer prayers and sacrifices at the temple. Although neighbour-ing city-states frequently waged war on one another, they also banded together in certain circumstances under the leadership of the strongest chief. Confederation of the seven chiefs on Puná Island and of a number of Cara Phase towns are men-tioned by Spanish writers as precipitated by threats of Inca domination. Although confederation was apparently volun-tary, centralization of authority was effective enough to offer severe resistance to the Inca armies. More than one battle ended in an Inca defeat, no small achievement in view of the enor-mous disproportion between the manpower, organization and supplies commanded by the Inca generals and the Ecuadorians.

CHAPTER VII

The Inca Conquest

THE HIGHLANDS

Fig. 49

THE INCA CONQUEST of Ecuador began between 1463 and 1471, when the southern highland basins of Loja and Cuenca were incorporated into the Empire by Topa Inca. His son, Huayna Capac, extended the northern frontier to the present Ecuador-Colombia boundary after his succession to the throne in 1493. The conquest of the Cara is said to have taken 17 years and required a series of bloody battles, in which the Inca armies more than once fled in defeat. Inca resources of manpower were superior, however, and victory was ultimately theirs. To punish the Cara for resistance, Huayna Capac ordered the capture and execution of all who had fought against him. Whole villages of survivors were moved to the region south of Cuzco, their populations replaced by loyal subjects from that area.

The system of *mitimaes*, or colonists, not only destroyed local solidarity and thus inhibited rebellion, but also speeded up effective integration of the newly conquered zones by introducing a core of settlers accustomed to the laws by which the Empire was governed. Consolidation was further promoted by immediate construction of administrative centres and extension of the Inca highway, which was acclaimed by Cieza de Leon who had travelled the Roman roads in Spain as 'the finest road to be seen in the world'.[5] Along this road, messages were carried by relay runners from Quito to Cuzco, a distance of 1980 km., in eight days. Local chiefs were absorbed into the administrative hierarchy, the Inca language (Quechua) and religion were made compulsory, and tribute was levied according to the special resources of each region.

The principal administrative centres in Ecuadorian territory were at Tomebamba in the Cañari region, Riobamba and

Latacunga in the Puruhá region, and Quito and Caranquí in
the Cara region. Each contained palaces, sun temples, ware-
houses, and nunneries accommodating some 200 virgins, all
erected of fitted stone masonry. Along the road connecting
these major centres were rest houses, fortresses, and additional
storehouses. Tomebamba became the favourite residence of
Topa Inca, and of his son Huayna Capac, who was born there.
Its magnificence astounded Cieza de Leon, although it was
already in ruins when he saw it:

> These famous lodgings of Tomebamba . . . were among the
> finest and richest to be found in all Peru, and the buildings
> the largest and best. Whatever the Indians said about these
> residences fell short of reality, to judge by the remains. . . .
> The temple of the sun was of stones put together with the
> subtlest skill, some of them large, black, and rough, and
> others that seemed of jasper. . . . The fronts of many of the
> buildings are beautiful and highly decorated, some of them
> set with precious stones and emeralds, and, inside, the walls
> of the temple of the sun and the palaces of the Lord-Incas
> were covered with sheets of the finest gold and incrusted with
> many statues, all of this metal. The roof of these buildings
> was of thatch, so well laid that barring a fire, it would last for
> ages. Inside the dwellings there were sheafs of golden straw,
> and on the walls carved figures of the same rich material, and
> birds, and many other things. In addition to this, it was said
> that there was a great sum of treasure in jugs and pots and
> other receptacles, and many rich blankets covered with silver
> and beadwork. Whatever I say, I cannot give an idea of the
> wealth the Incas possessed in these royal palaces, in which
> they took great pride . . .'[6]

If it were not for such eye-witness accounts, it would be difficult to demonstrate that the Ecuadorian highlands were integrated into the Inca Empire. All of the massive Inca stone

Fig. 50

buildings were in ruins less than 25 years after Pizarro first sighted Ecuadorian soil, and today hardly a trace remains. The hill-top fortress of Ingapirca, near Cañar, is the only important exception. Evidence of Inca contact is provided by aryballoid jars found throughout the highlands but most frequently in the south, closest to the Peruvian border. Canteens, *keros* (flat based, flaring walled cups), jars with a horizontal loop handle placed high on one shoulder, and other diagnostically Peruvian vessel forms also made their appearance in the southern highlands during the late period. Historical evidence informing us of the Inca system of interchanging populations permits us to suggest that these introductions were made by colonists brought from the Titicaca Basin, but in earlier periods similar evidence has been more cautiously interpreted as implying trade relations rather than political domination. This situation highlights the difficulty of inferring supranuclear political integration from archaeological remains.

THE COAST

The Spanish chroniclers are in agreement that the Inca never succeeded in integrating the Ecuadorian coast into the Empire. Estete, who accompanied Pizarro on his third trip, drew the boundary as follows:

> From Tumbez begins the peaceful domain of the lords of Cuzco and the good land; and although the lords we have left behind and he of Puná who was a great chief were their subjects, they were not as docile as from Tumbez southward. They only offered recognition and certain tribute and nothing more. But from Tumbez southward all were vassals and very obedient.[7]

Although the coastal Indians spared no efforts to maintain their freedom, their success was probably due more to the en-

Fig. 50. Inca aryballoid with atypical appliqué in the form of a snake, a common element in Milagro Phase art

vironment than to their military prowess. After the open terrain of the highlands and the Peruvian coast, the forests and large rivers were unappealing to the Inca, and their efforts to incorporate such regions can only be characterized as half-hearted. Their failure resembles efforts of more recent civilized armies to overcome forest dwellers when forced to engage them on their own ground. It is a measure of the wisdom of the Inca rulers that they refused to pursue the matter to unprofitable lengths, dignifying their withdrawal by the judgment that the inhabitants were unworthy of their attention.

Archaeological materials of Inca origin are very rare on the coast. Even the omnipresent aryballoid jars are seldom reported. An intriguing exception is an Inca grave excavated by Dorsey on La Plata Island. Grave goods included five metal figurines (three of gold and one each of copper and silver) of typical Inca style, copper bells, pottery vessels of Inca forms and a gigantic stone axe, suggesting a person of considerable importance. Perhaps he was one of the generals who led the reconnaissance of the coast in the time of Topa Inca.

END OF THE PREHISTORIC ERA

By a tragic coincidence, Huayna Capac died in Quito in 1527, the same year that Pizarro first sighted the Inca Empire at Tumbez. The two events may not be unrelated, since the Inca ruler was a victim along with some 200,000 of his subjects of an epidemic disease probably of European introduction. Almost immediately, the Ecuadorian highlands became a battleground in the struggle for supremacy between the legitimate heir, Huascar, and his half-brother Atahualpa, who usurped command in Quito. The Cañari were the first casualties. Approached by both sides, they chose loyalty to Huascar, for which they paid severely when Atahualpa won. The civil war continued until Huascar's death in 1532 after a final contest near Cuzco. By a second coincidence, 1532 was the year in which Pizarro returned to undertake the conquest of Peru. No time remained to restore the equilibrium of the Empire, and it was more vulnerable than it had been for decades.

In Ecuador, the consequences of the Spanish discovery were swift and devastating. By 1547, the Indian population of Manta was reduced to 50 and Atacames, where 10,000 warriors met the first explorers, was abandoned. An early census of the Guayas basin lists less than 1800 Indians, of whom 1000 were children under 18 years of age. No major battles are recorded, and the decimation largely reflects the silent victory of European diseases to which the Indians had no natural immunity. In the highlands there was more resistance, but many lost heart when Cotopaxi erupted in 1534, signifying the displeasure of the gods. One foreign master was exchanged for another, but the wanton destruction and tyranny of the Spanish provided a cruel contrast to the order and justice that had prevailed under the Inca. Cieza records 'seeing with my own eyes old Indians who, when they came within sight of Cuzco, stood looking at the city and making a great outcry that afterwards turned to tears of sadness, contemplating the present and recalling the past,'[8] and it cannot be doubted that this sentiment was widely shared.

The accomplishments of the Inca in the Ecuadorian highlands were so impressive, and their rewriting of history so successful, that the conquistadors and many who have followed them have been misled into the belief that prior to their coming the Indians were little more than savages. Archaeological investigations are only beginning to uncover the truth, but what is already known places the Inca in their proper perspective as the next to the last of a series of foreigners whose influence was blended into the indigenous culture. Thus to restore extinct cultures and forgotten peoples to their rightful place in history is one of the most satisfying accomplishments of the archaeologist.

Text References

1 Saville, 1907, pp. 19–20.
2 Cieza de Leon, 1864, p. 179.
3 Cieza de Leon, 1864, p. 180.
4 Sámanos, 1844, pp. 196–197 (translated from the Spanish).
5 Cieza de Leon, 1959, p. 138.
6 Cieza de Leon, 1959, pp. 69–70.
7 Estete, 1938, p. 213 (translated from the Spanish).
8 Cieza de Leon, 1959, p. 186.

Select Bibliography

There is no up-to-date summary of Ecuadorian archaeology in English or Spanish. Many of the primary sources are in Spanish, published privately or in outlets with limited distribution outside Ecuador. Even monographs once more widely available are now out of print. To complicate further the search for information by an interested outsider, results of much of the fieldwork undertaken during the past decade are still unpublished. References listed here provide a guide to more detailed information on some of the archaeological phases, and several contain bibliographies that can be consulted for additional reading.

For a comparison of cultural development in Ecuador with that in other parts of aboriginal Latin America, as well as an appraisal of continent-wide interrelations, see:

MEGGERS, BETTY J. and EVANS, CLIFFORD, Editors. *Aboriginal cultural development in Latin America: An interpretative review* (*Smithsonian Miscellaneous Collections,* vol. 146, no. 1). Washington, D.C. 1963.

CHAPTER I

FERDON, EDWIN N., JR. *Studies in Ecuadorian Geography* (*Monographs of the School of American Research,* no. 15). Santa Fé, 1950.
MILLER, E. V. 'Agricultural Ecuador', *The Geographical Review,* XLIX, 183–207. New York, 1959.
WOLF, THEODORE. *The Geography and Geology of Ecuador.* Toronto, 1933.

CHAPTER II

BELL, ROBERT E. *Archaeological Investigations at the Site of El Inga, Ecuador. Casa de la Cultura Ecuatoriana,* Quito, 1965.

CARLUCI, MARÍA ANGÉLICA. 'Puntas de proyectil', *Humanitas,* IV, no. 1, 5–56. Quito, 1963.

KRIEGER, ALEX D. 'Early Man in the New World', in *Prehistoric Man in the New World* (Jesse D. Jennings and Edward Norbeck, *Eds*), 23–81. Chicago, 1964.

STEWARD, JULIAN H. 'The economic and social basis of primitive bands', in *Essays in Anthropology presented to A. L. Kroeber,* 331–350. Berkeley, 1936.

CHAPTER III

MEGGERS, BETTY J., EVANS, CLIFFORD and ESTRADA, EMILIO. *The Early Formative Period on Coastal Ecuador: The Valdivia and Machalilla Phases (Smithsonian Contributions to Anthropology,* vol. 1). Washington, D.C., 1965.

ZEVALLOS MENÉNDEZ, CARLOS and HOLM, OLAF. *Excavaciones arqueológicas en San Pablo: Informe preliminar.* Guayaquil, 1960.

CHAPTER IV

COE, MICHAEL D. 'Archeological linkages with North and South America at La Victoria, Guatemala', *American Anthropologist,* LXII, 363–393. 1960.

COLLIER, DONALD and MURRA, JOHN V. *Survey and excavations in southern Ecuador (Field Museum of Natural History, Anthropological Series,* vol. 35). Chicago, 1943.

EVANS, CLIFFORD and MEGGERS, BETTY J. 'Formative Period cultures in the Guayas Basin, Coastal Ecuador', *American Antiquity,* XXII, 235–247. 1957.

CHAPTER V

BENNETT, WENDELL C. *Excavations in the Cuenca region, Ecuador (Yale University Publications in Anthropology,* no. 35). New Haven, 1946.

BERGSØE, PAUL. 'The metallurgy and technology of gold and platinum among pre-Columbian Indians', *Ingeniørvidenskabelige Skrifter,* nr. A 44. Copenhagen, 1937.

—— 'The gilding process and the metallurgy of copper and lead among the pre-Columbian Indians', *Ingeniørvidenskabelige Skrifter,* nr. A 46. Copenhagen, 1938.

BUSHNELL, G. H. S. *The archaeology of the Santa Elena Peninsula in south-west Ecuador.* Cambridge, 1951.

COLLIER, DONALD and MURRA, JOHN V. *Survey and excavations in southern Ecuador (Field Museum of Natural History, Anthropological Series,* vol. 35). Chicago, 1943.

DORSEY, GEORGE A. *Archaeological investigations on the Island of La Plata, Ecuador (Field Columbian Museum,* publ. 56). Chicago, 1901.

ESTRADA, EMILIO. *Arqueología de Manabí central (Publ. del Museo Víctor Emilio Estrada,* no. 7). Guayaquil, 1962.

ESTRADA, EMILIO and MEGGERS, BETTY J. 'A complex of traits of probable transpacific origin on the coast of Ecuador', *American Anthropologist,* LXIII, 913–939. 1961.

ESTRADA, EMILIO, MEGGERS, BETTY J. and EVANS, CLIFFORD. 'The Jambelí culture of south coastal Ecuador', *Proceedings of the U.S. National Museum,* vol. 115, 483–558. Washington, D.C., 1964.

EVANS, CLIFFORD and MEGGERS, BETTY J. 'Relationships between Mesoamerica and Ecuador', in *Handbook of Middle American Indians* (Robert Wauchope, Editor), vol. 4. Austin, 1966.

D'HARCOURT, RAOUL. 'Archéologie de la Province d'Esmeraldas (Equateur)', *Journal de la Société des Américanistes,* n.s. XXXIV. Paris, 1942.

JIJÓN Y CAAMAÑO, JACINTO. *Puruhá Contribución al conocimiento de los aborigines de la Provincia del Chimborazo, de la República del Ecuador.* Quito, 1927.

UHLE, MAX. 'Estudios Esmeraldeños', *Anales de la Universidad Central,* XXXIX, no. 262. Quito, 1927.

CHAPTER VI

At the end of the Integration Period, historical documents become available to supplement the archaeological record. Those who described

Indians of the coast include Francisco de Jerez and Pedro Sancho de la Hoz, who accompanied Pizarro and served successively as his secretaries; Miguel de Estete, a soldier, with Pizarro on his third trip; Juan de Sáma⁄ nos, who has preserved the descriptions of a Manteño raft captured by Bartolomé Ruiz in 1527, and Agustin de Zárate, who became treasurer⁄ general in Peru in 1543. For the highlands, the best authority is Pedro de Cieza de Leon, who travelled throughout the Andean region between 1532 and 1550. Only those chroniclers quoted in the text are mentioned below:

CRUXENT, J. M. 'Noticia sobre una estación arqueológica: Hacienda Pucará, Ecuador', *Antropológica*, no. 1, 33–39. Caracas, 1956.

ESTRADA, EMILIO. *Los Huancavilcas, últimas civilizaciones pre⁄históricas de la costa del Guayas* (*Publ. del Museo Víctor Emilio Estrada*, no. 3). Guayaquil, 1957.

—— *Ultimas civilizaciones pre⁄historicas de la cuenca del Río Guayas* (*Publ. del Museo Víctor Emilio Estrada*, no. 2). Guayaquil, 1957.

FERDON, EDWIN N. JR. 'Reconnaissance in Esmeraldas', *El Palacio*, XLVII, no. 12 and XLVIII, no. 1. Santa Fé, 1940–41.

HUERTA RENDÓN, FRANCISCO. 'El Museo de Oro de la Casa de la Cultura del Guayas', *Vistazo*, VI, no. 81. Guayaquil, 1964.

MEGGERS, BETTY J. and EVANS, CLIFFORD. 'Archaeological evidence of a prehistoric migration from the Rio Napo to the mouth of the Amazon', *University of Arizona Social Science Bulletin 27, 9–16*. Tucson, 1959.

SÁMANOS, JUAN DE. 'Relación de los primeros descubrimientos de Francisco Pizarro y Diego de Almagro, sacada del códice número CXX de la Biblioteca Imperial de Viena', *Colección de Documentos Inéditos para la Historia de España*, tomo V, 193–201. Madrid, 1844.

SAVILLE, MARSHALL H. 'Antiquities of Manabí, Ecuador. Preliminary Report', *Contributions to South American Archeology*, I. New York, 1907.

—— 'Antiquities of Manabí, Ecuador. Final Report', *Contributions to South American Archeology*, 2. New York, 1910.

VERNEAU, R. and RIVET, PAUL. *Ethnographie ancienne de l'Equateur*. 2 vols. Paris, 1912.

CHAPTER VII

CIEZA DE LEON, PEDRO DE. *The travels of Pedro de Cieza de Leon,* A D *1532–50, contained in the First Part of his Chronicle of Peru.* Hakluyt Society Edition. London, 1864.

—— *The Incas of Pedro de Cieza de Leon.* Norman (Okla.), 1959.

ESTETE, MIGUEL DE. 'Noticia del Perú', *Biblioteca de cultura peruana,* Primera serie no. 2, 195–251. Paris, 1938.

JIJÓN Y CAAMAÑO, JACINTO and LARREA, CARLOS MANUEL. *Un cementerio incasico en Quito y notas acerca de los Incas en el Ecuador,* Quito, 1918.

Sources of Illustrations

All photographs are by Clifford Evans, except for Plates 24, 33, 64–65 and 69, which are courtesy of the Smithsonian Institution.

Drawings are by George Robert Lewis; those redrawn from publications are as follows: Bell: 5 a–e; Carluci: 5 f; Bushnell: 24 b; Dorsey: 26, 30; Estrada and Meggers: 32; Saville: 37; Huerta Rendón: 40e; Verneau and Rivet: 43, 44, 46, 48; Cruxent: 45; Jijón y Caamaño: 47; Jijón y Caamaño and Larrea: 50.

THE PLATES

3

4

9

10 11

12

13

14

15

16

17

18

19

20

21

22

23

24

25

26

27

28

29

30

31

32

33

34

37

38

39

40

41

42

43

44

45

46

47

48

49

50

51

52

53   54

55

56

57

59

60

61

62

63

64

65

66

67

68

72

73

74

75

76

Notes on the Plates

1 View toward the mouth of the Río Esmeraldas and the modern town of Esmeraldas, at the base of the ridge on the left. Formerly forested, much land has been cleared for pasture. The low area on the right is inundated during the rainy reason.

2 City of Manta from the ridge flanking the valley on the south. Refuse from Bahía and Manteño Phase occupations underlies the modern houses in the low area and extends over the ridge in the foreground.

3 The bay of Valdivia on the coast of Guayas Province. The modern fishing village occupies the beach, while refuse of the Early Formative site of the same name covers the slope in the foreground.

4 Fishing village of Puerto de Chanduy on the Guayas coast. The Manteño Phase site on the higher tongue of land may have had a similar appearance when it was inhabited.

5 Typical xerophytic vegetation of cactus and scrub at the edge of Lagarto salitre on the Guayas coast between Playas and Posorja. Such salt flats, which occur along the coast of Guayas Province, have replaced mangrove swamps and tidal inlets in existence when the archaeological sites were inhabited. Shell midden refuse of Jambelí Phase origin covers the elevated area at the right.

6 Otavalo region at the southern end of the Ibarra basin, north highlands of Ecuador. Cultivated fields continue up the slope of Imbabura, the summit of which is lost in clouds.

7 Highland terrain between Quito and Otavalo. Step-like fields on the steep gulley slopes are possible because the porosity of the volcanic soil minimizes run-off and consequent erosion.

8   The Río Napo on the eastern lowlands. The irregularly shaped patches in the forest are abandoned field clearings in various stages of secondary growth.

9   Valdivia Phase tetrapod bowl with a red-slipped surface and incised decoration. Both form and decoration are typical of Period A. Diameter about 25 cm. Early Formative Period.

10 Sherds of early Valdivia Phase decorated types. a–b, excision; c, finger-pressed rim; d, g, broad incision on polished surface; e–f, h–j, incision on unpolished surface; k–l, finger-pressed rows; m, p, multiple drag-and-jab punctation; n, rocker stamping; o, finger grooving.

11 Sherds of decorated types of Jōmon pottery from the Japanese islands of Kyushu and Honshu. a–b, excision; c, finger-pressed rim; d, i, broad incision; e–h, k, incision on unpolished surface; j, finger-pressed rows; l, rocker stamping; m, finger grooving; n, multiple drag-and-jab punctation.

12 Valdivia Phase pottery figurines of the earliest or Valdivia type. The recessed flat face, long neck and carefully executed coiffure are typical. Height of the complete example, 9·2 cm. (one leg missing). Early Formative Period.

13 Pottery figurines of the San Pablo type, characteristic of Valdivia Phase Period C. The face projects above the plane of the hair, the neck is shortened, coiffure is simplified, and the back of both head and body is plain. Height of the complete example on the right, 7·2 cm.

14 La Chorrera, a habitation site on the left bank of the Río Babahoyo, occupied during the Late Formative, Regional Developmental and Integration Periods. The bottom of the excavation is at the original ground surface. A large part of the site has been swept away by the river, which rises several metres during the rainy season each year.

15 Sherds from open bowls decorated on the interior by iridescent painting, an unusual technique characteristic of the Chorrera Phase. Late Formative Period.

16 Zoomorphic vessel with spout and bridge handle, probably dating from the Late Formative Period on the Ecuadorian coast. Height about 18 cm.

17 Stirrup-spout jar from the Cuenca basin, southern Ecuadorian highlands, probably dating from the Formative Period. Height about 21 cm.

18 Spouted jar combining a human head with an animal body and decorated with zoned red painting and incision. Probably late Chorrera Phase. Height about 24 cm.

19 Guangala Phase bowl with red painted decoration on a polished buff surface. Depth about 13·6 cm. Regional Developmental Period.

20 Pottery vessel in the form of a house. The upper wall and small door are painted red, while the rest of the surface is natural buff. The cylindrical spout (partly broken off) gave access to the hollow interior. Height to ridge about 13 cm. Tejar Phase, Regional Developmental Period.

21 Guangala Phase bowl painted red and black on polished buff. Depth about 7·5 cm. Regional Developmental Period.

22 Seated figurine with elaborate head-dress. Height about 27 cm. Jama-Coaque Phase, Regional Developmental Period.

23 Hollow pottery figurine with incised and red painted decoration. Height about 24 cm. Guangala Phase, Regional Developmental Period.

24 Cylindrical jar with a Chone type standing figure on one side. Height about 33 cm. Jama-Coaque Phase, Regional Developmental Period.

25 Chone type figurine of a kneeling woman. Height about 26 cm. Jama-Coaque Phase, Regional Developmental Period.

26 Hollow figurine of the La Plata Seated type, showing typical arm and leg position, ornaments on nose, ears, arms and neck, and small double beard. Face modelling is unusually realistic in comparison with other

Bahía Phase figurine types. Height about 21·5 cm. Bahía Phase. Regional Developmental Period.

27 Male figure seated on a four-legged bench. Beaded collar, arm and leg bands are typical ornaments on Jama-Coaque Phase figurines, but the head-dress is unusual. Height about 26 cm. Regional Developmental Period.

28 Mould-made figurine of a seated animal with elaborate head-dress and collar. The green painted face has the Chone D-shaped eye. Height about 12 cm. Jama-Coaque Phase, Regional Developmental Period.

29 Almond-eyed female figurine with naturalistic treatment characteristic of the Tolita Phase. Vertical yellow and red stripes decorate the skirt. Height about 15 cm. Regional Developmental Period.

30 Tolita Phase male figurine seated on a cylindrical stool. He holds a small jar in his left hand and an unidentified object in his right hand. Height about 13·5 cm. Regional Developmental Period.

31 Left: Mould for a pottery mask or figurine face. Right: Mould for movable pottery figurine head. The neck fits into a circular opening in the body. The wrinkled forehead and cheeks occur on many figurines of the north coast. North coast, Regional Developmental Period.

32 Top left: Fanged monster head with green and yellow post-fired painting. Height about 12 cm. Jama-Coaque Phase. Top right and bottom: Fanged monster heads from La Tolita. Regional Developmental Period.

33 Sphinx-like figurine. Height about 18 cm. North coast, Regional Developmental Period.

34 Left: Pottery mask with holes through the centre of the eyes and three small perforations along the upper edge. The exterior is white slipped. Height 12·5 cm. Right: Pottery plaque, perforated along the upper edge for attachment. Height 10 cm. Jama-Coaque Phase, Regional Developmental Period.

35 Pottery roller or cylindrical stamps with complicated patterns. Length 6–8 cm. Jama-Coaque Phase, Regional Developmental Period.

36 Flat pottery stamps with circular or asymmetrical outline and abstract or zoomorphic patterns. Diameter of circular examples at left, 5–7 cm. Jama-Coaque Phase, Regional Developmental Period.

37 Jar with the upper portion modelled in the form of a house with upswept gables. Negative painting covers the lower body. Height about 27 cm. La Tolita, probably Integration Period.

38 Pottery model of a house on a platform with steps at the front. The upper part of the roof is hollow and the gables rise to high peaks at the front (tip missing) and back (completely missing). A figure may have been seated in the doorway as on Figure 32a. A green band outlines the entrance, and the gable front is painted red. Height about 24 cm. La Tolita, Regional Developmental Period.

39 Pottery head-rest with double column support. Length of base, 13·4 cm. Jama-Coaque Phase, Regional Developmental Period.

40 Pottery head-rest with double column support and reclining figure on the base. Bahía Phase, Regional Developmental Period.

41 A large Milagro Phase platform mound, part of a complex south of Yaguachi, in eastern Guayas Province. This structure, about 100 metres long and 10 metres high, is surrounded by numerous small house mounds and several large cemetery mounds, constituting one of the major urban centres of the Milagro Phase. Integration Period.

42 A chimney burial, one of a large number revealed during levelling of a Milagro Phase burial mound on the Babahoyo river. The lower jar contained a secondary burial with relatively few grave goods. The chimney is constructed of similar jars with the bottoms knocked out, inverted one above the other and sealed at the junctions with blue clay. Integration Period.

43 Twisted-leg tripod vessel with rare appliqué fillet decoration. Height about 15 cm. Milagro Phase, Integration Period.

44 Bifurcated-leg tripod jar with decoration produced by a three-pointed comb. Height about 20 cm. Milagro Phase, Integration Period.

45 Small vessels with ornate appliqué of birds, frogs, snakes and human figures, probably with ceremonial significance. Height about 10 cm. Milagro Phase, Integration Period.

46 Two forms of Milagro Phase pedestal bowls or compoteras. Height 10 and 17·5 cm. Integration Period.

47 Deer effigy vessel with negative painted decoration. Body length about 18 cm. Milagro Phase, Integration Period.

48 Small bone and stone carvings of human, bird and animal figures. Largest about 4 cm. long. Milagro Phase, Integration Period.

49 Left: Anthropomorphic amulet carved in soft whitish stone. Height 7·7 cm. Right: Stone amulet composed of a human figure with a snake on his back. Height 6·9 cm. Milagro Phase, Integration Period.

50 Set of 12 earrings, each constructed of a single continuous piece of gold wire. All are from the same chimney burial, suggesting that they were worn six on each ear, probably spaced along the outer margin. Length about 4.3 cm. Milagro Phase, Integration Period.

51 Fragment of brown and white cotton textile with a warp float pattern. Milagro Phase, Integration Period.

52 Fragment of a cotton garment with silver dangles attached in rows, from the burial urn of a person of high status. Milagro Phase, Integration Period.

53–5 Plaques of solid copper with bird-like or anthropomorphic faces at the upper end. These come from burial urns and may be symbols of wealth or status. Length about 26 cm. Milagro Phase, Integration Period.

56 Left: Tall goblet with a flaring, horizontally fluted neck, rounded body and flaring base. Height 17·8 cm. Centre: Tall goblet with fluted cylindrical body and flaring base. Height 20·3 cm. Right: Tall goblet with walls in-curving slightly to constricted mouth. Height 23·6 cm. Manteño Phase, Integration Period.

57 Pedestal-based bowls with polished surfaces and incised decoration. Height about 9 cm. Manteño Phase, Integration Period.

58 Small balsa raft used by modern fishermen off the southern Guayas coast, probably similar to those used during the prehistoric period.

59 Polished black vessel in the form of a duck. The orifice is in the top of the head. Manteño Phase, Integration Period.

60 Manteño Phase compotera with negative painted decoration on a polished orange surface. Height about 16 cm. Integration Period.

61 Typical Manteño Phase anthropomorphic jar with burnished line decoration on the body and a mask-like face appliquéd on the neck. Height about 46 cm. Integration Period.

62 Manteño Phase anthropomorphic jar showing the typical grotesque profile. The surface is highly polished black, except the face. Height about 25 cm. Integration Period.

63 Hollow pottery figurine (restored) of a style more commonly depicted in stone. Manteño Phase, Integration Period.

64 Stone seat of the kind encountered at Manteño Phase sites in the Manabí hills. Height 73 cm. Integration Period.

65 Manteño Phase stone mortar in the form of a feline. Height about 13 cm. Integration Period.

66 Tall jar with negative and red painted decoration. Height 67 cm. Cara Phase, Integration Period.

67 Small polished jars with embellished shoulders. Diameters about 14·5, 12 and 11·8 cm. Cara Phase, Integration Period.

68 Bowls painted with narrow red bands smeared by subsequent horizontal polishing of the surface. Diameters about 15·5 and 12 cm. Cara Phase, Integration Period.

69 Red and white painted anthropomorphic jar. The right hand holds a small trophy head. The bulging cheeks of the vessel face, which probably represent chewing of coca quids, are also shown on the trophy head. Ambato region, probably Integration Period. (The necklaces of shell beads were not on the vessel originally).

70 Red slipped and negative painted bowl interior. Diameter about 22·4 cm. Puruhá Phase. Integration Period.

71 Left: Tripod jar with *hoja de cabuya* legs. The form is typical of the Puruhá Phase, but the surface is covered with a green post-Spanish glaze. Height about 16 cm. Right: Tall compotera of a Puruhá Phase shape coated with green post-Spanish glaze. Height about 19 cm. Integration Period.

72 Anthropomorphic burial urn in the form of a warrior holding a shield. The white slipped surface has black and red painted decoration. The opening is in the bottom. Height about 34 cm. Napo Phase, eastern Ecuador.

73 Napo Phase burial urn with stylized anthropomorphic facial features and polychrome painting in pseudo-negative style. Diameter about 33 cm. Integration Period.

74 Rim fragments illustrating typical incised and excised decoration of the Napo Phase. Integration Period.

75 Square basin with intricate red and black design painted on the white slipped surface. Low relief on the rim repeats the double-headed snake

motif on the interior. Width about 47 cm. Napo Phase, Integration Period.

76 Napo Phase vessel with black-on-white painted decoration and a cam-bered or trough-like rim. Height 34 cm. Integration Period.

Location of objects illustrated in the Plates

Museo Víctor Emilio Estrada, Guayaquil, Ecuador: Plates 9, 12, 18, 20–23, 25, 27–32, 35–37, 39, 43–50, 53–55, 59–63, 73;
United States National Museum, Washington, D.C.: Plates 13, 15, 26, 33–34, 38, 51–52, 64, 66, 69, 74–76;
Museum of the American Indian, Heye Foundation, New York: Plates 16, 19, 56–57, 67–68, 70–71;
Baltimore Museum of Art: Plates 24, 65;
Portoviejo, Manabí school: Plate 40;
Casa de la Cultura Ecuatoriana, Quito, Ecuador: Plate 72.

Index